REMEMBER THE BEATLES SINGING "WHY DON'T WE DO IT IN THE ROAD?"

NOW XAVIERA SHOWS YOU HOW TO DO IT ANYWHERE, ANYTIME, WITH ANYONE YOU WANT.

Only Xaviera Hollander would have dared have sex:

—*with a taxi driver in his cab at noon in Central Park*

—*on an escalator at Bloomingdale's*

—*with a politician who demanded his wife play the part of a lesbian*

—*with a woman schoolteacher who turned Xaviera into a rapturous pupil*

—*with a father-and-son combination in the most arousing erotic competition of Xaviera's life*

Now Xaviera lets you in on the secrets and the fun of following the wildest flights of erotic imagination to the most unforgettable seX-periences of a love-lifetime!

XAVIERA'S FANTASTIC SEX

SIGNET Books You Will Want to Read

☐ **XAVIERA ON THE BEST PART OF A MAN** by Xaviera Hollander. Now the Happy Hooker lays it all on the line to share the joy of sex with you, recreating the lessons she's taught as well as the equally fascinating lessons she's learned in her intimate dealings with—THE BEST PART OF A MAN. (#E7848—$2.25)

☐ **XAVIERA'S SUPERSEX: Her Personal Techniques for Total Lovemaking** by Xaviera Hollander. An ultra-erotic tour through the world of sex by someone who has tried it all—every sensual possibility available to men and women of every sexual taste and level of expertise. A lavish, large-format bedside companion with 50 exquisitely erotic illustrations. (#G9967—$5.95)

☐ **HOW TO BE THE PERFECT LOVER** by Graham Masterton. Make love erotically—in ways you never thought of before. The book that tells you all you need to know to be the perfect lover. (#W6674—$1.50)

☐ **HOW TO DRIVE YOUR MAN WILD IN BED** by Graham Masterton. From the author of How to Be the Perfect Lover, exciting new erotic techniques to achieve the ultimate in sexual pleasure. (#E7850—$1.75)

☐ **SECRET SEX: Male Erotic Fantasies** by Tom Anicar. If you think your private sex fantasies are pretty kinky, wait till you read this fantastic collection of the secret sexual desires of men of every erotic taste. (#E6946—$1.75)

THE NEW AMERICAN LIBRARY, INC.,
P.O. Box 999, Bergenfield, New Jersey 07621

Please send me the SIGNET BOOKS I have checked above. I am enclosing $_____(check or money order—no currency or C.O.D.'s). Please include the list price plus 35¢ (50¢ for Xaviera's Supersex) a copy to cover handling and mailing costs. (Prices and numbers are subject to change without notice.)

Name_____

Address_____

City_____State_____Zip Code_____
Allow at least 4 weeks for delivery

XAVIERA'S FANTASTIC SEX

by

Xaviera Hollander

A SIGNET BOOK
NEW AMERICAN LIBRARY
TIMES MIRROR
A BERNARD GEIS ASSOCIATES BOOK

NAL BOOKS ARE ALSO AVAILABLE AT DISCOUNTS IN BULK
QUANTITY FOR INDUSTRIAL OR SALES-PROMOTIONAL USE.
FOR DETAILS, WRITE TO PREMIUM MARKETING DIVISION,
NEW AMERICAN LIBRARY, INC., 1301 AVENUE OF THE
AMERICAS, NEW YORK, NEW YORK 10019.

COPYRIGHT © 1978 BY ROYALTY HOLDINGS, N. V.

All rights reserved

SIGNET TRADEMARK REG. U.S. PAT. OFF. AND FOREIGN COUNTRIES
REGISTERED TRADEMARK—MARCA REGISTRADA
HECHO EN CHICAGO, U.S.A.

SIGNET, SIGNET CLASSICS, MENTOR, PLUME AND MERIDIAN BOOKS
are published by The New American Library, Inc.,
1301 Avenue of the Americas, New York, New York 10019

FIRST SIGNET PRINTING, FEBRUARY, 1978

1 2 3 4 5 6 7 8 9

PRINTED IN THE UNITED STATES OF AMERICA

Contents

I.	Introduction: Bigger than Life, and a Whole Lot More Fantastic	1
II.	The Once and Future Fling	9
III.	A Role in the Hay	47
IV.	Xaviera's Fail-Safe Fantasy Kit	80
V.	Who's Afraid of the Big Bad Fetish?	125
VI.	Xaviera's Magic Mail	157
VII.	The Washington Capers, or Federal Fantasies from My Forbidden File	182
VIII.	Seven Fantastic Sex Scenes You Can Play	215

I. Introduction: Bigger than Life, and a Whole Lot More Fantastic

I was telling an old boyfriend about my orgasm with a banker under my mink coat, on an escalator in Bloomingdale's, when I noticed his complexion turn remarkably pale. What's wrong? I wondered. Had I said something to upset him?

"How could you even think such a thing?" he gasped and took a step back.

"Well, it's only a fantasy," I said, trying to explain myself. But he was too shocked.

"Xaviera, I don't care!" he exclaimed. "That doesn't sound very nice."

Nice? "Nice?" I asked, not quite believing him. "Who wants sex to be nice? It should only be *fantastic!*"

My last book, *Xaviera's Supersex*, was for your body; I showed you numerous ways of increasing your repertory of sex techniques to achieve my special brand of "Supersex." Now I give you those sex techniques that will expand your erotic imagination into the realm of my "Fantastic Fantasy Sex."

George Bernard Shaw once wrote, "The more things a man is ashamed of, the more respectable he is." And if there's one thing respectable people are ashamed of, it's their own sex fantasies. If you ever want to devastate a party of uptight people, just start talking about your bondage fantasies or incestuous dreams. The whole party will come to a halt, and so will the flow of invitations from your host. I know because it's happened to me.

I was attending a cocktail party in Montreal about the time Warren Beatty's *Shampoo* was being released. I'd seen and loved the movie, but one very proper woman at the party was condemning it. "And that scene where Julie Christie wanted to crawl under the the dinner table," she shrieked, "what poor taste!"

I was curious to know why this episode upset her, and so I said, "I thought it was very funny."

"Funny," she gasped, "I don't see anything so funny about Julie Christie wanting to . . . to *do* Warren Beatty right under a dinner table!"

"Do him?" I asked. "You mean, give him a blow job?" The room was immediately quiet except for a few audible gasps. "Why, one of my greatest fantasies is to suck guys off under tables, at the fanciest restaurants in town. In fact, I've acted out this fantasy at dinner parties many times—for free."

I'd promised my host I wouldn't talk about my sex life, but how could I resist? I, for one, don't believe that sex fantasies should be kept in people's closed mind or between book covers. They should be shared with others, and wow, am I going to share my fantasies with you in this book! Surprisingly, many liberated authors have written sex guides that see fantasies as nothing more than safeguards against sex crimes. The psychiatrist Dr. Peter Dally, in his book *The Fantasy Game*, writes that sex fantasies "are an important safety valve, allowing us to imagine that we are doing or saying things that in reality are forbidden and/or impossible." Nancy Friday has expressed this same philosophy in her writings, and even my dear friends the sexologists Drs. Phyllis and Eberhard Kronhausen have written, "There is a widespread belief that sexual fantasies are apt to lead sooner or later to acting-out in real life. But for the average individual, even the wildest and most anti-social sex fantasies serve only . . . to keep actual behavior within socially tolerable limits."

The message seems to be: Think about it, let your dreams run wild, but for chrissake, don't ever do it!

Of all our professional sexologists, only Dr. William Masters (*Human Sexual Response*) offers a slightly more progressive view: "All of us use fantasy, to a greater or lesser degree. It is a form of self-stimulation. It helps us move from where we are to where we want to be, when the occasion warrants. In that sense it is a bridge and can be very useful."

But how do you build those bridges from fantasy to reality? First, look upon fantasies as part of your everyday experiences—the shadow to their substance. They are not a substitute for the real thing; rather, they are an integral part of real life. And please don't call yourself weird or perverted for dreaming up the wildest sex scenarios. Fantasizing is a creative process and should be accepted as such.

Fantasies as scenarios—that's what sex is all about. To show you want I mean, let's begin with those fantasies you can actually enact or, as I prefer calling them, "dreams to come true." Everyone's sex life begins with this kind of fantasy. As an adolescent schoolgirl I used to dream of kissing my girlfriends' mouths. Fantasies would run through my head of teasing the schoolboys so that their crotches would grow and bulge. Without first playacting these fantasies in my head, would I ever have gotten together with either sex?

Not that these sex fantasies should stop with the loss

of your virginity! I receive dozens of letters every month from inexperienced women who fantasize about oral sex. I've talked to men who, dreaming of their childhood days, want their girlfriends to enact spanking scenarios with them. You can never be a child again, but is that any reason you can't pretend you *are* a child—and a naughty one at that—once in a while? If you're newly married, you may dream of swinging and orgies and partner swapping. In time, your fantasies can lead you to experiment.

If you've already realized that fantasy can become a healthy and useful part of your sex life, try some sophisticated role-playing in bed. A drag queen once told me, "Darling, you are what you wear," to which I added, "You are what you *dare*." For instance, your boyfriend may be a powerful, successful businessman or politician who wants to be dominated. In the privacy of your bedroom, you can help him realize his impulses through sadomasochism, bondage, or even transvestism. (Why not try on his pinstriped suit for a change and play the aggressor?) Rape fantasies may be played out between you and your spouse, but don't be afraid to switch roles occasionally. In fantasies, the man doesn't always have to be the "rapist."

For example, fantasy role-playing not only enhanced but actually helped save a relationship of mine. One of my girlfriends back in the States was a young college coed. We were so different. I was something of an exhibitionist, while she was very shy and retiring, but through our fantasy scenarios we were able to reach a sexy compromise. We would play this scene in which we were two college cheerleaders performing in a pep rally for her old alma mater. Neither of us was wearing panties under our cheerleading skirts, so when we jumped up and down our pubic hair showed. As we bounced around, we spread our legs so wide that absolutely nothing was left to the imagination. We were cheering at both ends! In our imagination, that is. Of course, we performed this fantasy in the privacy of our bedroom. We called it "the gay touchdown" routine. In this fantasy the student body was there watching us and cheering our "flashing" performance. We would then go into a tumbling routine in which we fingered each other ecstatically. The shock value of lesbianism in jock heaven—the old college football field—was enough to make me come. And it accomplished as much for my shy coed friend. You can try playing it when the men are watching Saturday afternoon football. If you can also lure them away from the TV set, it's a whole new ball game—but your team scores either way.

You say you're one of those who actually streaked naked across a football field? Then try delving into those fantasies that are just for the mind or what I call "creaming the impossible dream." Since my own repertory or *real* flesh-and-blood sexual experiences and partners read like lurid fantasy to most other people, you can imagine that my favorite fantasies are truly far-out—those that are impossible to enact. But why, you may ask, should I bother with mere libidinous dreams when I have so much of the real thing? Why? Because dreams are sometimes better than reality. And certainly a whole lot kinkier. And fantasy dreams can make real sex even sexier. When I'm alone, I sometimes masturbate, thinking I have a big penis between my legs—an impossible dream if ever there was one. But how do you expect to get ahead if you don't dream a little?

Even "impossible" fantasies, however, can be shared with others. Like the time an English film actor and I discovered that we were both into "lewd food." We fantasized that our sex organs were pieces of delicious fruit. When the actor parted my vagina and began licking my lips, he sighed, saying, "These are the best-tasting orange slices I've ever had the pleasure to devour."

Now, of course, I'd fantasized penises as bananas or carrots, but vaginas as oranges? Avocados, maybe, or figs. But oranges? How delicious! How unusual! How fantastic a fantasy. And so, his fantasy got my imagination working.

During our next evening together I dropped a little orange lozenge into my vagina before we made love. By the time he was performing cunnilingus on me, the lozenge had completely dissolved—but the orange flavor lingered on. My little trick so helped to enhance this actor's fantasy that he just went wild, slurping up all those great-tasting love juices. When he got down to giving me his fruit punch, the effect wasn't lost on me either, and I've loved banana daiquiris ever since. I also felt just that much closer to this guy for having the trust and openness to share his secret fantasy with me. Sometimes you have to be a bit fruity to have fun.

As this episode shows, sex fantasies can help enhance sex that's already good. There are those times, however, when you just can't get it on with your bed partner and your fertile imagination is your last recourse. A few months ago I had just this kind of experience. I was sleeping with a London stockbroker I'd known before becoming the "happy hooker." Whenever he'd arrive in town for a quick business deal, we'd get together for a lengthy session in bed. The sex had always been great in the past, but this time around it just wasn't the same. Nothing worked. Finally, I looked up at him and said, "What's the matter? Can't you think of anybody else either?" At that we both cracked up. The ice was broken at last, and we could get down to some real business. And I'm not referring to Dun & Bradstreet.

Perhaps our sex wouldn't have begun so badly if I'd been more honest with the broker from the start. That evening with him I wanted an orgy; one man wasn't enough for me. If I'd told him this right off, maybe we could have fantasized some wild bacchanalian affair together and spared ourselves a lot of meaningless pumping and puffing. Everybody has fantasies, so sharing them with others is synonymous with having an open and honest relationship. And what better way to expand your own repertory than by exchanging fantasies with others.

People tell me, "Xaviera, I don't have your crazy imagination. I can't dream up all those weird fantasies." The problem here could be that you're trying too hard and looking in the wrong direction. Forget about those astronauts screwing green Martians or a hundred penises hopping around on your front lawn. These are simply too abstract and foreign. I've found that the most erotic fantasies are those that closely relate to your own environment and past experiences.

If you're interested in creating better fantasy scenarios, begin by reliving some of your own childhood wet dreams. Sigmund Freud wrote that our sexual makeup is already determined and set by age five, and as any child psychologist knows, kids have infinitely more active sexual imaginations than we adults care to believe.

As a schoolgirl, I remember feeling warm pangs vibrate from my crotch every time my father laid me across his knee and spanked me. Now that I think back, did I feel his erection during those spankings—or was it only his keys? Did my hair fetish begin when my dear God-fearing mother read me tales of Samson and Delilah from the Bible? I've had many Americans tell me that the cartoon series *Popeye and Olive Oyl* was a favorite machismo sex fantasy during their kindergarten years. Personally, when it came to sadomasochism I preferred the bubble-gum wrappers with the big stud kicking sand in a ninety-pound weakling's face. I was always the girl who left the weakling for the muscle man.

I'm often told, "But, Xaviera, when I have these crazy fantasies—sex fantasies of intercourse with my sister or having my ass whipped—how can I share them with others? They'll think I'm a weirdo and reject me." It's simple. Just guide the conversation so they begin to tell you *their* fantasies. Soon you'll be returning the compliment—and the next thing you know you may be making a duet of those dreams, at least in modified form.

If you don't have someone with whom you can share fantasies, be my guest. This book is dedicated to you, and in it I'm going to share my wildest fantasies, and those of my friends, with you.

II. The Once and Future Fling

Telling your sex fantasies to someone else is the most difficult thing in the world to do if you are a novice fantasist. Althought I believe in sharing fantasies with others, sometimes it just isn't necessary—or wise—to tell others about your secret sex life in order to make it all come true. Just do it and keep your mouth shut. If you're attending your first orgy or seducing your first lesbian, no one else has to know you are not a veteran at the game. For instance, the woman who wants sex in the backseat with a taxi driver shouldn't ask the cabby, "You know, I've always fantasized about making it with somebody in a cab. Could you please oblige me?" No, the cabby need not know you have a fetish for men in yellow cars. Just seduce him as you would anyone else—off the meter, of course.

Sex fantasies have a way of coming true, and if you dream about them long enough, the circumstances for making them come true will eventually arise. So be prepared for that once and future fling!

Like Father, Love Son

The family that lays together stays together? Well, maybe not, but there are situations that can bring family members (and other kinds of members) closer together, as you'll see shortly.

One of my favorite sex fantasies has always been intercourse with a father and his son at the same time, anally and vaginally. It's also one fantasy you *can* enact, if the circumstances arise—which they have for me on several occasions. In fact, my first sex upon returning to Holland was a nice cozy family three-way.

In the summer of 1976 I left Toronto and flew back to Amsterdam to live with my mother for a while. I was being deported from Canada and did not look forward to the prospect of life back in Europe, but I soon made the adjustment to my old European surroundings. The Dutch newspaper columnists covered my return, and as soon as my name and picture hit the newsstands, former lovers and old school friends began calling me for dates. Soon it was as though I'd never left.

I hadn't seen most of these people since I left Holland in 1967, and one of these old acquaintances was a boss of mine at a secretarial agency. Although we'd never shared the same bed, Jon and I were pretty good office buddies in the two years we worked together. So many men are condescending to their secretaries, treating them like servants, but Jon was different. He was considerate and kind—and not bad-looking either. At times he even confided in me about his family and personal life. When I left Holland, he was in the middle of a very messy divorce from his wife, and although I used to wish he'd make a pass at me, I didn't push it because I didn't feel he was much interested in me. Or so I thought at the time.

We'd lost contact when I moved to the States, so you can imagine my surprise when only two days after I returned to Amsterdam I received a phone call from Jon. Jon Milton? I couldn't even place the name at first. After all, it had been almost ten years. Then I remembered. What was he doing now?

"Divorced. Single. No longer working for the agency. Set up my own business. How about a date? See you at Towne's Pub tonight at eight? Okay." A date with Jon Milton? I couldn't believe it.

Jon Milton. My God, he'd be older now, but so was I. We'd never even touched each other, and now I had wild fantasies running through my head about the one who got away. Jon Milton—the big unfulfilled lay of my life! Just thinking about seducing him after all these years got me hot, so hot that I had to masturbate myself with the electric toothbrush before I could even consider getting ready for dinner. He sounded so sexy over the phone, but . . . but maybe he just wanted to chat over old times. If that was the case, I'd just have to seduce him. *If* I found him attractive, of course.

I can't remember taking so much time preparing my makeup as I did that evening. I'd been so depressed since leaving Toronto, but now my spirits were high just thinking about this fantasy of unconsummated love . . . no, make that *lust!*

I arrived at the Towne Pub ten minutes early; usually I'm fifteen minutes late. When Jon walked in—he was five minutes early—we recognized each other immediately. He hadn't changed that much, more distinguished perhaps, with gray hair now. You wouldn't call him a hunk, but Jon was a fairly large man, and age hadn't affected his body for the worse.

We started talking, and we had so much to catch up on that the words just poured out. Jon was even more courteous than I remembered. I'd always appreciated that quality in him, his politeness and courtesy, but now I also found him to be very sexy. After five minutes of conversation I knew I wanted us to make love that night. I prayed that my fantasy was mutual, and then awhile later, just as I'd hoped, he asked me to his apartment around the corner.

"Why, of course," I said, "I'd just love to see your Hundertwasser prints." What a line, I thought, but who cares when you're horny.

I couldn't get over how excited I was by this man. Obviously, my dreams of invading old forbidden territory had gotten my sex drive running overtime. Evidently, it couldn't have been more mutual, for we just tore away at each other's clothing the minute we got to his bedroom. Our kisses weren't kisses—it was almost as if we were raping each other's lips. There couldn't have been more than five minutes of foreplay, and rough foreplay at that, before Jon entered me. A few thrusts of his erection, and I was already climaxing. Two minutes later, and he was coming with me. You couldn't call it premature ejaculation, really it was more what you'd call a delayed reaction—like ten years delayed—and we were both just too hot to hold back and savor our lusty sex. Anyway, there's nothing wrong with a quick climax if your man can get it up for a second go-around.

Jon asked me to give him another fifteen minutes and "I'll be back in shape."

"How about thirty?" I gasped. "I don't think I could

handle anything like that again in just fifteen minutes!" He laughed. Even though our sex had been faster than a rabbit, it was the most ferocious lovemaking I'd experienced in a long while. Well, since leaving Canada at least.

The two of us were lying there naked, trying to recuperate, when I heard someone fiddling with keys at the front door. My God, what was this? Had Jon remarried? Was his wife returning home unexpectedly? He hadn't said anything. Oh, why did my real-life fantasy have to end this way—with a jealous wife chasing me out of her bed!

"Jesus," Jon hissed between his teeth. "Martin's home early."

"So who's Martin?" I asked, grabbing for my scattered clothing.

"Don't get excited." Jon laughed. "He's not my boyfriend. It's just my son. You remember Martin, my kid."

I'd completely forgotten that he had a son. Of course, when I last saw Martin, he was only seven. I relaxed a little, but I still wasn't too happy about the situation. Family settings aren't usually conducive to uninhibited sex, and if Martin was going to embarrass Jon right out of another erection, the kid sure had bad timing.

I heard father and son talking about something in the living room, but I couldn't quite make it out. Their voices were too muffled, but it did seem that Jon was trying to coax his kid into doing something. What I didn't know. Finally, Jon got back into bed with me. His penis wasn't hard yet, and so I began munching on his earlobe. He pulled me away, though, and said, "Look, Xaviera, we've had great sex, but you've got to do me a favor. Our sex has been so good that I'd like to share it with my son."

My tongue dropped halfway out of my mouth. "With your son?" I asked breathlessly.

"Yeah, you see, he's seventeen now, and my God, the kid is still a virgin." Jon looked almost embarrassed. "You'd be doing him a real favor," he added.

"But, Jon, I'd really rather do it again with you," I said. "No offense to your son, but I don't know him." As if that had ever stopped me before.

"Oh, don't worry about that," he said. I could see Jon was awfully eager. "I'll be doing it along with him. Martin will be up front and I'll be in back."

"Oh, like an airplane trainer," I said.

"Yeah, like an airplane tr—" He paused. "Well, you know what I mean, Xaviera. Come on, please, for me and the kid?"

I thought for a moment. I'd made it with a father and his son only six times before. The last one was well over a year ago, too, and each one of these incestuous sessions had been fantastically good sex. I'd gotten hot many a time just thinking about them, so why not again? And if there's one thing I like better than an experienced stud, it's a virgin. With his hot father in back and innocent Marty up front, why, I'd have the best of both worlds. Fantasies have a way of coming true, if you just wait long enough.

Jon had already poured Martin some whiskey, and when we were introduced his son was drinking it as if it was Kool-Aid—and he was nervous enough to need all the Kool he could get. I asked him if he'd like to sit next to me, which he did, and as I slowly began undressing the boy, I commented on what a beautiful body he had. The kid actually was a bit skinny for my taste, but he wasn't bad either: lots of bushy black hair and rather well-developed arms and legs—for a youngster his age. But the big surprise came when I pulled off his dark-blue boxer shorts and saw his huge, gorgeous erection flip up in my face. A guy should have a license to carry something like that, and this kid hardly had a learner's permit!

I glanced over at Jon. His eyes registered complete surprise; then they kind of glazed over as he stared mutely at his son's beautiful erection, Martin's penis had to be at least two inches longer than his father's and much, much thicker. The veins were just popping out all over that kid's good, husky shaft. Jon's just couldn't even compare. And Jon knew it, too. Where, I wondered, did this boy get his cock? It certainly wasn't from Jon's side of the family. The two men kept glancing back and forth at each other's organs, and I could just feel the rivalry begin to develop between them. Yes, this would be unusual sex, indeed.

I started sucking on Martin's big erection. My ass was stuck up in the air, and I felt Jon grease me up with some Vaseline. His hard-on slid into me, and I wiggled my hips around to take all of him up into me. Then Jon and I sat back together, me on top of his erection, so that his son could enter my vagina from the front.

The kid was so nervous he couldn't even aim his erection in the right direction. Jon kept trying to calm him down, telling him how good my hot vagina would feel when he finally stuck his virgin hard-on into me. I couldn't say anything; I just kept looking at that big thing between that skinny kid's legs. I was literally coming at the thought of his entering me. Of course, having his father's penis up my ass helped. Jon was already humping away in back, and his thrusts coupled with the sight of Martin's heroic erection got me so excited that I just had to start masturbating my clitoris. Finally, I grabbed Martin's hard-on and stuffed it into my box.

It felt so good! As good as I thought it would feel.

Even after I had had so much tumultuous sex only thirty minutes before with his father, the boy's erection just filled me up completely. I wasn't expecting much from Martin as a lover, this being his first time and all, but with his father thrusting up my ass, Martin gradually began to pick up on Jon's beautiful rhythm. Soon they were meeting each other's thrusts head-on, and I could feel their penises hit and slide together within me.

"Can you feel your father's hard-on, Martin?" I asked. Martin could only nod yes, but he continued giving it to me, sliding his erection into me alongside his father's.

"Jon, how about you?" I asked. "How does your son's erection feel in me?"

"Beautiful," he groaned. And his penis didn't miss a beat of his son's.

The two continued screwing me as though they were waging a contest to see who was the better lover. My body was their arena, and I was the referee.

Who won? Well, this was probably the first athletic contest in history in which the referee was the indisputable victor.

The Jock's on Her

My favorite customers as a madam and call girl were always the sports car racers. Of all the sporting men I've known, these guys had to be the most intelligent, the most adroit and controlled of lovers, and they possessed all the masculine sexual finesse in the world. Many women, however, prefer their sporting men to have some kind of physical contact with their opponents. Sara was one such call girl, who would laugh at me for my fantasies about race car drivers. "Who wants a man who just sits in a car?" she used to say. "You might as well get yourself a taxicab driver," to which I'd say, "Well, what's wrong with cabbies?" (Read my following fantasy entitled "My Fare Lady." No, there's nothing wrong with cabbies!)

Sara's idea of the ultimate athlete was a hockey player. "Now there's man-to-man combat for you," she'd say. I'd never attended a hockey match before, and since Sara was always talking about how great the players were—in bed and on the ice—I asked her once if she'd mind my going with her to one of these matches.

"Oh, Xaviera," she said with a sigh, "you'll just love it. But you won't believe those men. They're literally gods on ice!"

Sara was so excited when we entered Madison Square Garden for the game I was just hoping I wouldn't be disappointed by this "spectacle of manly combat," as she called it.

When the players skated out onto the rink, I had to admit that they were plenty masculine, even though it was difficult to tell about their builds under all that padding. But the match itself? Well, somehow, I was expecting more athletics and something less in the way of hand-to-hand and stick-to-stick combat. This wasn't a game—it was war! Men punching away at each other, getting hit with hockey pucks, breaking sticks, and starting fights! It was so violent that I couldn't even watch three-fourths of the match, but Sara . . . well, Sara was in ecstasy. Some of the heavier bondage and SM freaks in my clientele used to request Sara's services, and now I could see why she was such a favorite. This girl ate up every moment of that hockey match, particularly all that out-and-out combat. When one defenseman threw himself up against an opponent, I thought Sara was going to have an orgasm, and as the fight began with both teams at each others' throats, she went wild along with the crowd. Madison Square Garden was suddenly one big emotional orgy with everybody getting their rocks off on this violence. Personally, I'd have preferred my hockey players making love between the sheets rather than waging war on a sheet of ice.

You can imagine how surprised I was two weeks later when I received a phone call from a member of this very hockey team, asking if he could engage the services of my brothel. "There'll be about eight of us," he said, "all from the team, and we'd like eight girls. All in the same room, if you have one large enough. You know, an orgy-type situation."

The team was to show up the every next night. Usually Sara didn't come to my brothel on Friday nights—her night out with a financé—but I called her up anyway. I knew she wouldn't want to miss this one. "Friday night?" she asked. "Oh, damn, I can't pass up this chance. I'll just have to meet Gary's parents and family some other night. Don't worry. I'll be there. You know I will."

Sara was a real athlete groupie. She'd balled with every kind of professional jock imaginable. "But never, but never," she screamed over the telephone, "have I ever been invited to an orgy with a whole goddam hockey team!" Not only that, I reminded her, but she would be making a few hundred dollars to boot. "I'm going to get paid for this?" she asked. I was almost afraid her question was serious.

"Of course, you're getting paid!" I snapped back.

"This is business." And then I laughed. I was never the kind of boss who discouraged fun on the job.

The night of the big orgy Sara refused all services for other customers. "I've got to save myself for the boys," she kept saying. And every ten minutes she would ask me when they were coming. "They are coming? You're sure of this now?"

When they finally did arrive, Sara practically collapsed on the sofa. Soon every girl in my place was begging to be a part of this orgy, and I was almost afraid a fight might break out among my call girls. I couldn't really blame them either, for even my experienced eyes were impressed by these athletes. Even without all their hockey gear and padding, they were very impressive specimens indeed. These were definitely big, husky, men with lots of muscle and the kinds of shoulders you only dream about. I hadn't planned to make it with these hockey players, but why not? Maybe Sara knew something I didn't.

These eight guys were members of the No. 1 hockey team in its division. Needless to say, they were successful as hell, and tonight they had just won a big match and wanted to celebrate. The best liquor, all the grass and hashish I could provide, they didn't really care how much it all cost. These eight men wanted to get good and stoned and then have the wildest orgy we girls had ever experienced.

After they had drunk and smoked enough to make an entire army pass out, I led them to my largest bedroom, which contained king-size beds, and put on some hard rock music. I asked them if they wouldn't prefer a little privacy, even some screens to separate the beds, but no. It was team spirit all the way. "We want an orgy," said the team's captain, between tokes on the water pipe. "We all wanna be in the same room, in the same scene with the same girls. Give us eight chicks, and each and every one of us will take our turn on every one of them."

And so eight of us joined these big burly jocks for a go-round on my two king-size beds for the orgy of our lives. Sara was so excited she was already experiencing orgasms just rubbing her legs together. When a muscle-bound goalie grabbed her and mounted and entered her with absolutely no foreplay, I could see her lifelong fantasy flash before her eyes in living, breathing Technicolor.

"Oh, give it to me hard," she moaned. "Score me, baby! Score me, baby!"

And did he ever score her! I mean, this goalie shot his wad into Sara in a record thirty seconds.

"Hey, boys," he shouted. "I came first. I came first. I made it. I'm the winner!"

All the other jocks gazed over at him, looks of disappointment crossing their faces. It seemed they all wanted to achieve the first orgasm. How often, I thought to myself, had I worked with inexperienced men, trying to prevent them from shooting their cum too soon. And here these big masculine jocks were, making sex just another hockey game. All they knew how to do was to shoot the puck into the goal, and the opposition be damned. Coming first was simply another way of scoring for them. I had never known premature ejaculation to be anyone's fantasy, but it was exactly what these hockey players wanted in an orgy situation.

Immediately the other players started thrusting their hard-on into us as though there were no tomorrow. Were they trying to make up for lost time? "Well, if I can't be first," one of them grunted, "I sure as hell can make second place." And about twenty seconds later his penis was spending itself inside me. So much for the female orgasm!

Contrary to what many sexologists say, most johns

really do want their prostitutes to experience an orgasm. But not these hockey players! As each guy achieved his orgasm, shooting his cum off into whatever girl he happened to be screwing, he would yell it out so that the other players would know. When the last player came—in a mere ten minutes!—they called time-out.

"Now let's see who can get the first hard-on," one of them screamed, and sure enough, the first man with an erection scored five points. When they had all recuperated, it was the same old ball game. First orgasm, and you score ten points.

Needless to say, Sara's fantasy of hockey supersex was ruined. "I've made it with these guys individually, and the sex has been great," she said afterward. "But together, they've got this sex fantasy that they're a bunch of pubescent little boys jerking themselves off with our bodies."

But the athletes did enjoy themselves, and over the next few months they had a number of orgies at my brothel and various hotel rooms around New York City. Generally, their fantasy of who-scores-first was a crashing bore for any horny prostitute, and after a few sessions with them most of my girls took it as just another job. Myself? Well, give me a good cabdriver any night of the week.

My Fare Lady

Erica Jong immortalized sex between strangers with her "zipless fuck" in *Fear of Flying*. Of course, while Ms. Jong was coining catchy phrases at her typewriter, many more of us were actually cashing in on those zipless fucks and certainly had no fear of flying with whatever stranger we happened to choose.

Sex with a stranger is probably the ultimate fantasy trip; you can make this nameless person into whomever you want. He's just a face without a name or a personality, an empty canvas waiting to be colored and sketched. I think this is one reason why so many horny women are attracted to prostitution; it gives you ample opportunity to have sex with absolute strangers. And if you have an avid imagination, the sex can be fantastic.

While I never had any qualms about mixing pleasure with my business, when it came to fantasies about strangers, I preferred picking up my own men, and life in New York City certainly gave me that opportunity. What other place in the world so depends on the kindness of strangers cruising the streets in taxicabs for their next fare? I must have taken at least a thousand cab rides while living in New York, and although some of those cabbies lived up to their seedy reputation—cigar-smoking, combative, irritable, and downright rude—a lot of those men on wheels were among the city's finest.

Sex with a cruising cabby? I must have enacted this

backseat, fare-ticking fantasy dozens of times. Of course, not every cabby provided a happy experience. That's the problem with enacting fantasies; you take your chances. Sometimes that cute stranger behind the wheel in the front seat looks awfully inviting through the rearview mirror, but when he joins you in the back, he's just plain awful. The good, the bad, and the ugly. Enacting fantasies is not for the weak of heart, but if you've got a spark of courage, it's worth the candle.

One of my more memorable "improper strangers" was a cabdriver I met on my way home from my lawyer's offices on Fifth Avenue. At the time I was involved in a rather ugly lawsuit with one of my publishers. A book of mine was selling incredibly well, yet my royalties were downright paltry. My lawyer and I decided to sue, and while we were eventually successful, it took a long fight in court to get my rightful money. It was about nine o'clock at night when I left his offices this particular summer evening. Although my apartment wasn't that far away, I was just too weary to make the walk, so I tried getting a cab.

Fifth Avenue was uncommonly quiet that hot August night. Why, I wondered, wasn't I out on Fire Island like everybody else? It took me a few minutes before I could hail an empty taxi. Sex was the last thing on my mind, and I didn't even look at the driver when I got into his cab.

"Fifty-fourth Street between Lexington and—" I stopped in midsentence. The driver's reflection in the rearview mirror—it caught my attention. I couldn't believe how handsome he was!

"Yes, ma'am," he said in a pleasant, deep voice. "Where can I take you tonight?" He actually sounded cultured.

"Oh, Fifty-fourth Street between—" I stopped again. I was so tense from haggling with my lawyer over old contracts and papers. I needed a release, a sexual release, and this driver was young and educated, and he had a dark, rugged face with a streak of cruelty running across it. Not malevolent, mind you, just a touch of evil as though he'd be good in bed—maybe even better in the backseat.

"Yes, ma'am? Where to?"

"Oh, I'm sorry," I apologized in my thickest Dutch accent. "Please, could you just take me for a ride through Central Park? I'm a visitor here, and I have to leave town tomorrow. I've heard so much about the park, and yet I just didn't have time to see it."

"Sure thing, ma'am," he said. Cabdrivers like nothing better than passengers who want a long, leisurely drive through the park. "It's night, of course, but there's still a lot to see in Central Park," he added.

"I'm sure there is," and I wasn't referring to the squirrels and the trees. Oh, this fantasy always got me so excited. Will he accept? How do I pop the question? Would the sex be good? What kind of sex? Questions, questions.

"You know, there's this statue of an angel somewhere in here," I began.

"Oh, yes, Bethesda Fountain. You want to go there?" the driver asked.

"Bethesda Fountain! Yes. I've heard so much about that fountain. Take me there." I remembered there was a small parking area near the fountain. I'd had sex with more than one cabby there, and it seemed a favorite spot for other "auto" erotic devotees. Not a big parking lot, just a couple of other cars for protection to ward off the muggers.

"Well, here's your fountain." And the driver pointed out the window to Bethesda Fountain. He slowed down the cab, almost to a halt. I didn't give a damn for that stupid tin angel with water dripping all over her. Oh,

XAVIERA'S FANTASTIC SEX

that parking area was only a few yards away. Couldn't he speed up this crate?

"Keep on driving," I said, trying to be as calm as possible. "I just wanted to look at the lovely angel."

And then there it was—the parking lot! "Ah, wait," I shouted. "Please slow down. I didn't realize there were parking lots in Central Park. Pull in here. This is the smallest, the cutest little parking lot I've ever seen!"

The driver looked back at me, puzzled, but he pulled in anyway. He was so obedient. Would he obey me all the way? "I've never really noticed it before," he said nonchalantly.

"Why, there are other cars in here, too," I exclaimed. I was being so naïve that I had trouble keeping from laughing out loud. "Why, where are the people? I don't see any people in these cars. Oh, this is frightening. So frightening." And I reached forward and grabbed his shoulder.

"There's nothing to be afraid of, ma'am," he said, looking back at me. "Why these people are just"—our eyes met—"why they are just under"—my mouth opened ever so slightly—"under the windows"—I held his shoulder even tighter—"and on the seats"—we both breathed heavily—"and they are getting down and"—he got out of the car and joined me in the backseat—"enjoying themselves . . ."

So many Americans have fantasies about sex in backseats. I suppose it just shows you what a mobile people Americans are. Sex in drive-in movies, in a car on some lovers' lane, in the backseat of a Ford losing your virginity, Xaviera Hollander in a taxi with a New York cabby in Central Park. I guess sex on wheels is a typical all-American fantasy. Of course, my being Dutch and all, it's an acquired taste for me, but with this cabdriver I kept fantasizing that I was some wholesome American teenager. Perhaps my boyfriend and I had just left the high school dance. The pond next to our car wasn't in Central Park but rather some lake near a road where virgin girls were deflowered by their equally green jock boyfriends.

The car wasn't a yellow taxi. Rather, my boyfriend, had borrowed it from his father for the evening. And there we were in the backseat, the same backseat he'd ridden to church in the weekend before with his parents and kid sister. But we were there now, making love awkwardly, yet passionately. He didn't have all his clothes off. Even the cabdriver left his shirt on in case he had to make a quick exit—from the parking lot, that is.

My green cotton dress was actually white taffeta, and I didn't care if this guy soiled it or not. This was sex in the backseat of his father's car, and I was never going to be a virgin again!

"Fifty-fourth Street between Lexington and Third Avenue, please."

I was on my way home now. I still didn't know his name. We'd made love, ravaging each other's bodies, but now he was just my chauffeur. There's nothing like cruising with a cabdriver to bring out the latent "john" in a woman. And I did tip him well.

As I left, I think I heard him humming a few bars of "My Fare Lady."

Not a Leg to Stand on

"I was so upset when I broke my leg skiing," Jim wrote in his letter to me. "The doctor said it would be at least six weeks before I'd be rid of the cast. Work is no problem; I just sit at a desk all day anyway. But Xaviera! The cast runs from midthigh to my ankle. What about my sex life?"

What about his sex life? It hadn't been much to begin with. What now? Jim was a friend from Toronto, and since I'd moved back to Europe, we usually communicated with pen and paper. His work at a large insurance company was hardly the world's most exciting job, and I sometimes wondered whether or not his lethargy in bed stemmed from his job or vice versa. He was such a shy person, you couldn't help feeling sorry for his additional physical problems. If he wasn't aggressive enough to meet and make women under normal circumstances, I was sure it was twice as difficult to get things in motion now.

On further consideration, however, it occurred to me that occasionally mishaps such as Jim's can work to one's sexual advantage. I was ready to write him my condolences when I started thinking about that big, hard, thick cast of his. Casts? Ah! Now it was all coming back! I remember on some of my college lecture tours I'd occasionally see some big football-jock type limping around with crutches or with his leg in a cast. "Wounded in action," I'd asked, "or just from falling out of somebody's bed?" I felt bad about their injuries, of course, but the fantasy of that cast on some he-man type always got my libido working. After all, you might as well make the best of a bad situation. In my fantasy, the cast would end somewhere above the guy's knee. An inch or two of his big, muscled thigh would show, and then there'd be the penis, which almost seemed like an extension of all that rock-hard plaster. The fantasy of crawling into bed with a man and his cast just seems so erotic. Actually, it's a little like the fantasy of having a giant penis.

But with a cast the man is really rather helpless, and it's easy for me, the woman, to dominate—to control him and his orgasm. He's not the aggressor, thrusting away at my crotch. Now I create the rhythm of our lovemaking. Now it's me straddled over him, my knees on each side of his hips, my vagina suspended over his erection, taking it and sucking it up into me. My legs rub up against the plaster cast. His legs are now hard and rough where once they were soft and hairy, and it makes him seem even harder and larger in me. Maybe I even straddle his leg and rub my crotch up and down his cast; I dream that it's some penis on an ancient stone statue of some mythical Greek god. The statue is large and cold and carved out of marble, and I'm its goddess.

It's a simple fantasy, but one I've never experienced.

Why wasn't Jim here when I needed him? Or more to the point, why wasn't I with Jim when he needed me? Then I thought, so what if he's back in Toronto and I'm here in Amsterdam? A long-distance call was the least I could do, even if I couldn't offer my humble services in person.

As soon as I heard his voice over the transatlantic phone, I shouted my greetings and advice. "Casts are my biggest unfulfilled fantasy," I said. "Don't let it get you down. It's a blessing in disguise."

Jim burst out laughing. "I know, Xaviera, I know," he said. "This is the best break I've ever had. At first I thought this cast would make me a monk for two months. Not so. I've never screwed—or should I say, *been* screwed—so much in my entire life.

"You remember what a wallflower I was at all those parties? Well, I haven't changed, but now that I can't go to the girls, they come to me—and I do mean *come*! Believe me, Xaviera, you're not the only woman who has a thing about casts. At parties all the girls are attracted to me, some out of sympathy and some because they want to see what signatures are on my cast. I carry a pen now, and when I put my leg up for them to sign, they have to touch me. Usually they hang on to me around the waist or shoulders, or maybe they even put a helping hand on my hip. Do you realize how difficult it used to be to get a girl to touch me at a party?

"Now the girls pet me, cooing about how sorry they feel for me. When I tell them I broke the leg skiing, I can just see their eyes light up. A skier! How romantic. Of course, I don't tell them it was my very first time on the slopes.

"I remember one girl, this foxy chick named Sally. I swear every guy in that room wanted to have her, but she came right over to me, asked me how I broke the leg, and started autographing my cast. In no time I had an erection. I wasn't wearing any underwear either, since I couldn't get it over the cast. My erection just slid down my leg and reached the top of my cast. I don't think I'd ever seen it get that large before. It looked tremendous under those trousers.

"And here was this beautiful blonde rubbing her hand up and down the cast, just an inch away from my hardness. If she had spread her hand out, she'd have touched my erection. What could I do? I was ready to die of embarrassment. Of course, that got me even hotter, and my cock actually began to throb a little. I could see it twitch.

"By this time I just thought, what the hell? What do I have to lose? And so I asked her if she'd like to go to my place. She accepted—which surprised the hell out of me—and as she helped me up off the couch and into my coat, I think she noticed my erection. She giggled a little. Maybe it wasn't my bulge. Maybe she was laughing at my awkwardness. Like they say, women always go for the little boy in a man, and you really do feel kind of helpless and childish with these damned casts.

"When we got to my place, she undressed me and everything. Chrissake, I'm not *that* helpless, but you know, I've grown to like this geisha-girl treatment. I usually keep both my legs inside the bed, but in this case, I remember that I put my right leg—the one with the cast—outside the bed, with the foot up on a chair so that I didn't have much weight on it. Usually I'm the one who's on top, but this time Sally said, 'Just spread your legs, and I'll sit on top of you. Don't worry. Don't move your leg, but let me do it to you.' And she just sat right down on me, taking her weight on her knees. Sally even rubbed my cast—like on the couch—as though she was masturbating it. It's not the most active sex a man can have, but I'm sure getting a lot more of it."

Just thinking about that girl acting so aggressive and Jim being so passive and his cast being so hard got me really hot. What a great sex fantasy. I'd have given anything to have jumped a plane to have a go-round in bed with Jimmy and his cast myself. When I got the telephone bill a month later, I learned that I might as well have taken that plane. Why can't the phone company just get wise and install a dial-a-fantasy service?

An American Ream

One of the most common sexual games is to seduce someone who isn't interested in you. In fact, this desire is so common that we usually don't even think of it as being a fantasy—the fantasy of having someone we want but can't possess. For many people this attraction is even heightened if the other person is of the opposite sexual persuasion.

I remember trying to seduce one fortyish woman who I thought might be a lesbian. I met her at a party, and although she wasn't particularly talkative, she did seem knowledgeable about film. When I asked her if she'd seen the film *The Fox*, she replied yes, adding she enjoyed it very much.

"But what about those lesbian scenes?" I asked, trying to feign innocence. "Weren't you terribly shocked?"

"Why, of course not." She laughed. "Those things do happen, you know."

Her reply was so patronizing it almost made me ill. I thought to myself, I'll show her a thing or two about lesbianism, and so I put my hand on her shoulder and very tenderly kissed her neck. All of a sudden she swung around and slapped me hard across the face. "Don't you ever do that again," she cried, speaking between clenched teeth. And then she stomped across the room for another drink. I was stunned to hell, but I did learn a lesson: Don't play let's-lock-lesbian-loins unless you're prepared for the consequences. Until you've checked out your sources, it's a fantasy best kept in your head.

Still, there are those more adventurous than I. It's common for many heterosexual men to desire lesbians. Such straights will say, "I want to show her what a *real* man is like. I can make the dyke come." (I write about such a man, the Washington diplomat, in "The Washington Capers" chapter of this book.) Certain gay men are strongly attracted to straight guys whom they want to "bring out," as though every heterosexual man were just waiting to have his anus deflowered. This was the fantasy of a gay American photographer friend of mine whose studio was in Toronto. He did photographic assignments for some of the top Canadian publications, but as a sideline he would also shoot and develop nude pictures for people. In fact, he was particularly well known in the Toronto area for his home movies of orgies. "Give an orgy and have Danny shoot it for you," was his line, and it did become a very lucrative business for him.

I brought my friend Peter, a free-lance photographer, to one orgy Danny was shooting. Peter was new to Toronto, and I wanted him to meet Danny. Peter was just the opposite of Danny: Whereas Danny was very well established in the business, Peter was just getting started; Danny was gregarious, while Peter preferred being alone or with one person; Danny relished his gayness but Peter . . . well, Peter was very, very straight. In fact, he was disdainful of homosexuals. In other words, Peter was Danny's favorite fantasy, the untouched heterosexual male. And as a bonus, Peter was also well hung.

When Peter and I joined the orgy, I watched Danny's reaction as he got his first look at Peter's erection. Peter certainly was one of the most well-endowed men I'd ever known, and I was actually rather proud of showing off his male member to Danny—Danny who was always bragging about the large hard-ons he had taken.

Well, when Danny got a good shot of Peter's erection, he practically dropped his movie camera. It was obvious from the look of Danny's tongue that he wanted my man, and so just to tease him a little, I let him watch Peter and me ball. I just smiled as I took all that meat, humping and pumping and puffing a bit more than usual. It made a good show for Danny, too. Later that evening Danny told me he just had to have Peter in bed.

"Hands off," I warned with a sly grin. "This guy's straight, and I mean straight. No way will he ever make it with you."

Of course, this made Danny even more determined to fulfill his fantasy of having yet another heterosexual man. At the orgy I couldn't prevent Danny from introducing himself to Peter, and within no time they were talking about their photographic careers. Since Peter was a free-lance photographer and just visiting Toronto, Danny offered Peter the use of his equipment—his camera equipment, that is. Peter was virtually penniless, and he couldn't very well refuse; within a few weeks the two of them were working together on some photo assignments.

Danny had a way of trying to "help" Peter, which meant his elbow or his knee or his hand was always bumping up against Peter's large penis. But Peter was always very much against homosexuality and would say, "Danny, you're like my brother, but don't touch me." And Danny would say, "Oh, Peter, you're like *my* brother. You could put me right next to you in bed, and I wouldn't touch you." Naturally, Danny would be caressing and petting Peter's body all the while he was promising nothing more than brotherly love. "I wouldn't think of it," Danny used to say. "You're too dear a friend."

One evening I was supposed to meet Danny and Peter at the movies after a photography assignment they were working on. When we went into the theater to sit down, Danny looked at me with feigned pain, holding his ass. Of course, he was putting on an act, but I knew something had happened. And from the looks of things, it must have been something big! Peter was unusually quiet that evening, and this made me even more suspicious. So I asked Danny, "What happened?"

"I'm not allowed to say," he whispered back.

Now I was dying to get the story because Peter had always said, "No guy will *ever* screw me." Of course, he'd never said he himself wouldn't screw another guy. It wasn't until after the movie—unfortunately, a long double bill—that I was able to learn Danny's secret of how he had fulfilled his sex fantasy.

"Peter was very tired from tramping around town," Danny confided to me. "I cordially invited him to rest on the couch in my studio. I even gave him some sun blinders to put over his eyes to block out the light. You see, I didn't want him to see what I was going to do to his body!

"While he was resting, I put on some very soothing mood music that in the background contained the voices of two women in intercourse. Then I started rubbing Peter's back. He was so tired, and I'm such a good masseur—why, I just knew he couldn't refuse me. And he just sort of let himself go.

"We were listening to the record, and I said, 'Don't those two women sound hot?' I was trying to get his mind on *their* orgasm and off *my* hands. 'Boy, I really bet they have big boobs, too. Big asses, the kind you can sink your teeth into. Rubbing those big boobs up against each other, getting hotter and hotter, their crotches getting wetter and wetter. . . .' While I was talking dirty like that, I was working my hands lower and lower on his body. I started at his shoulders, but within a few minutes I was working his abdomen. By the time the two girls had reached their tenth orgasm I was soaking his crotch with baby lotion. I poured it all over his big penis and started working the daylights out of it. 'Don't those women sound excited?' I asked, trying to get his mind off my masturbating him. Finally, Peter was hard, so I just unzipped my pants and sat right down on that big hard organ of his. After a few thrusts of my pelvis that guy was so gone and so excited that he would have screwed anything alive, including vegetables."

And that's how Danny made Peter. The funny thing about this story is that Peter has always remained very secretive about it. To me, he still feigns disinterest in gay sex. I don't really think Peter is homosexual. Danny and he had sex together a few times after this, but as Danny put it, "He just came to me for sexual release. The less Peter could get girls, the more he'd come and visit me."

Eventually they both sucked each other off, and Danny even screwed Peter once. But after a few sessions together their mutual lust began to fade. Peter wasn't really into men, and after fulfilling his fantasy, Danny actually preferred his homosexual friends and their more open displays of gay sex.

They both gained from this experience, though: Danny acted out his fantasy, and Peter gained a new one. Prior to making it with Danny, Peter had always been very uptight about anyone's touching his ass. When we first met, I tried using my dildo on him, but he just looked at me in absolute horror and said, "You don't really use those things on men, do you?"—which can be a pretty disheartening thing to hear when you're greasing up your plastic for the evening. Many times I'd even tried going-around-the-world on Peter, but I only got so far. He loved blow jobs and having his balls sucked and licked, but just as soon as my tongue would stray to his anus, I could feel his body tighten up. Instantly he'd grab my head and lift me up from his crotch. Not even my littlest finger would be allowed entrance. But after Danny, Peter had been opened up to a "hole" new experience.

I didn't see Peter again until last year, when we were both visiting our families in Amsterdam. I gave him an autographed copy of my latest book, *Xaviera's Supersex*, and as he leafed through the pages, he stopped at the drawings of a woman using a big dildo on a man's anus. "This is one of my greatest unfulfilled fantasies," he said, staring at the sexy drawing.

I just smiled and whispered, "Unfulfilled? Not for long."

Blowing the Boys in Blue

Uniforms can be quite a turn-on for women, particularly for those females with a masochistic streak running through them. Why masochistic? Because uniforms generally connote power; they can automatically endow a man with an aura of authority. Naturally, the woman who gets off on men in uniforms—policemen, soldiers, guards—wants to feel inferior and humbled in the presence of these almighty studs in blue.

Personally, I've never been much attracted to uniforms, especially *police* uniforms. After running a brothel and having so many horrible dealings with policemen, the allure of badges and guns has been entirely erased from my sex drive. An acquaintance of mine, however, who is a big porno star in France, can't get her fill of cops. Stéphane loved to pick up her policemen right on the street, take them in a dark alley, drop their fly, and then screw them. She was probably the only girl I've known who liked policemen but was not masochistic. In fact, she was rather sadistic in her lovemaking, and even in her films, Stéphane usually played the aggressor and master—and I'm talking about triple X-rated sex, too. Since she was a porno film star, exhibitionism was also Stéphane's game, and it once happened that I was part of her voyeuristic audience as she took five—no, make that only four—policemen on the streets of Cannes, France.

I first met Stéphane some years ago when I was doing a whirlwind promotional tour through France for my first book. It was late in the afternoon and I was just finishing up a long and grueling day at a Parisian bookstore, autographing copies of *The Happy Hooker*. Stéphane walked into the bookshop. I didn't recognize her at first, though I should have, because only a week earlier I'd seen her latest porno flick, in which she played the madam of an SM whorehouse. Stéphane was causing quite a stir in the press because she had told everyone that this sex film was really autobiographical. She'd also written a book, a guide to sadomasochism, that was now selling fairly well.

The bald-headed little manager of the bookstore ran over to me when Stéphane walked in. He was all flustered, so much so that I could barely understand his French.

"Madam, this woman is Stéphane, the big film star," he said, his voice quavering. "This is my store. Please, please be polite." I guess he was expecting trouble from us, two celebrated sex symbols meeting each other head-on with no introduction.

The next thing I knew, there was Stéphane, all dressed in black leather with a big cape and hat, leering down at me as I signed autographs. Now, if we'd been civilly introduced, Stéphane and I probably would have got off to a much better start. After all, what did the manager think I was going to do? Bite her leg on the spot? If I'd planned to do that, I certainly would have had enough manners to wait until we got outside. True, I did feel intimidated by her austere presence and attitude. Just because my book was outselling hers was no reason for her to get naughty.

"So you are Xaviera Hollander, the famous madam and call girl," she said, speaking in a low, sexy French voice.

"My name is Xaviera Hollander," I said, "*author* and *lecturer*." And then I handed her a copy of my book, adding, "Would you like a taste of my talents? It's on the house."

The manager's eyes rolled skyward, and his hands quickly folded as though in prayer. What was he so worried about? I'd pay for the book.

"No, Miss Hollander," she began. "I'm not here to read your book. I've already had *that* pleasure. I'd like to invite you to a party I'm giving next week for my own book. Tomorrow afternoon I'll be here autographing the book. Maybe you can stop in for a copy, if you haven't already read it. The book is about sadomasochism; maybe you can use a taste of *my* talents."

I gulped. Actually I wasn't in the mood for leather

and chains. And so I did the only thing a civilized lady could have done under the circumstances—I lied. I said I'd read her book and found it very informative. Also, I was leaving for New York in the morning, and so, "Thank you very much, but I won't be able to attend your party." From the way she slammed and almost shattered the shop's glass door, I had a slight suspicion that she hadn't bought either of my stories—and for all I knew, she hadn't really bought my book either. Why, I wondered, were porno stars always so touchy?

I soon forgot about this episode with Stéphane, and I'm afraid the public forgot about her, too. Soon after, the French government began cracking down on pornography, and Stéphane could not make the adjustment to sex of a softer brand.

It wasn't until 1976 that the French censors began to relax again, making it possible for Stéphane's big comeback in a skin flick with herself as madam of an SM cowboy ranch—French jeans, of course. I didn't meet Stéphane again until I visited the Cannes Film Festival in the spring of '76. I was staying at a friend's chalet with a group of wild and sexy people. Everyone there was a swinger, and one of those who stopped by for some laughs and orgasms was Stéphane. She was in town to promote her hit film.

From the moment she entered the chalet, with two black Labradors in studded collars (Stéphane in her usual black leather), it was obvious that this girl was the ultimate exhibitionist. She just could not wind down from her on-screen life. "If I can't have a theater of people" she kept screaming, "then give me a bedful."

Well, she got a chaletful of swingers, which isn't bad. The swing went on at full tilt for some time, but finally, we all had screwed each other and knew each other intimately and we were all getting a bit bored with the same old faces, the same old bodies, the same old techniques, the same old . . . whatevers! One night we had all just had enough of one another, so we went into Cannes for a late dinner. We were staying in the mountains, and since we had only two cars, I drove one filled with five women (Stéphane included) and the five gents took the other. On our way back home we drove past the Boulevard des Anglais, and the big, fancy hotels in Cannes where the films were being played for the festival. The crowds of filmgoers and groupies and fans are just incredible around festival time, so the city has hundreds of extra policemen around these hotels.

Stéphane took one look at all those French cops and started yelling out the window, "My God, I want to pick up somebody. I want to get laid. It's two o'clock in the morning, and I haven't had any action yet." She pulled her head in and said to me, "There are three guys standing over there I haven't screwed. Pull over!"

I looked, but I didn't see any men. Just three cops. Oh-oh! Three cops! What the hell was this woman thinking of? Two of the other women in the car started getting nervous, but this one red-haired chick—a novice swinger—became curious. "Sex with a policeman?" the redhead said, her eyes bugging out. "I've never even dreamed of that!" Actually I was quite amused. Amused at the idea of Stéphane's wanting to have sex with a group of policemen *and* wanting to impress me so much. She had always wanted to be as big a celebrity as me, and even though her book sold sixty thousand copies (not bad), it was no *Happy Hooker*. But since Stéphane thought herself a big international star, she was going to show me how the pros did it. And so Stéphane staged an orgy with a few cops to entertain la Hollander.

At the time I was in one of those strictly voyeuristic moods. "Okay?" I asked. "What do you want me to do?"

"Slow down," she snapped back. "I want to pick up a policeman. Make that *five* policemen."

"That's fine," I said with a laugh, "but how are we going to—"

"Stop here!" Stéphane shouted, and I brought the car to a screeching halt. There on the curb were three policemen, young guys, very attractive-looking, standing around gazing at this carful of five crazy, horny women. Stéphane jumped out, introduced herself as the world's leading sex symbol, and led the three policemen down a dark back alley. I quickly grabbed the redhead from the car, and we followed Stéphane and the policemen.

Stéphane was the only one who was going to screw; my friend and I were just along for the show. She needed her audience, and we were it. And remember, I really wasn't into cops.

Stéphane was wearing a skirt and blouse, no bra or panties to slow things down, and it was no time at all before she had fucked and sucked all three cops. I'd never heard a woman laugh more between orgasms. Either she was giggling or coming.

"Come on, get me a couple more," she said with a laugh, ordering one of the younger policemen. "Get me two more of your colleagues."

In a few minutes, two other cops walked into the tiny alley for some quick sex with Stéphane. She pushed the first one up against the brick wall, lowered his trousers, and took him in a standing position. All the while she was shoving her pelvis against his, she played with the gun in his pocket. They could bring out the artillery, and they'd still be no match for Stéphane. She could keep them shooting for hours.

Well, there I was watching and keeping my distance when the other new cop came up to me and said, "How about you, *ma petite*? I want you, too." I guess Stéphane was such an easy lay this man felt he needed a challenge. Since I was holding back, he was getting pretty horny for me. I wasn't trying to play hard-to-get; I just wasn't interested in sex with a man of the law.

"No, please leave me alone," I said, trying to discourage him. But he just got more and more turned on. He even started pressing his crotch up against mine, and I could feel his erection.

"Hey, how about sucking my gun, mademoiselle?"

"Take her," I screamed, pointing to Stéphane. "Screw her." He started unzipping his trousers and waved his erection around at me as though it were loaded and ready to shoot—which I'm sure it was. I grabbed my companion's hand, and we got out of there—*fast*!

A few minutes later Stéphane came out of the alley with her five cops straggling in line behind her, and she was pissed off because the cop who wanted me hadn't screwed her. It seemed he couldn't have what he couldn't get, so he didn't want what he could get. I'd spoiled Stéphane's sex fantasy of having five policemen while a fellow sex symbol watched enviously.

Stéphane's fantasy was partly exhibitionistic, partly attraction to the police uniform, and partly sadistic. How was it sadistic? Well, unlike most women who enjoy sex with cops, Stéphane did not want the man in blue to dominate her. Instead, her fantasy was to so dominate the policeman sexually that she would actually humiliate him.

Since Stéphane never got her fifth policeman, I had somewhat spoiled her fantasy. "I was trying to break my record," she scolded me later.

"Four in one evening isn't the worst record in the world," I said, with a knowing glint in my eye. Indeed, lesser realities have fulfilled many a woman's fantasy.

Making it with five cops in a back alley in Cannes while an admiring audience cheers you on could be classified as an impossible dream. After all, even an international sex symbol like Stéphane couldn't quite bring it off. If your fantasies are really wild, you learn that a little bit of the real thing goes a long way. In other words, one cop in the sack is worth five in the alley—especially when five in the alley could get you five to ten in the slammer.

Potluck

Rest rooms have never seemed like an erotic setting to me. White porcelain and cold tiles—I've never exactly empathized with those who fantasize about anonymous sex in these places. The allure, however, is obvious: If ever there were a place built for the "zipless fuck," the rest rooms of the world are it. And not just for homosexuals either. Although many guys do other men in toilet stalls, there are some women I've known who actually plant themselves in a stall to wait for some unsuspecting man to occupy the adjoining compartment. Even more women fantasize being such an aggressive female, one who doesn't care what the consequences or who the man is. To those women, I dedicate this real-life "can fantasy."

Sex was the last thing on my mind when it all happened—I had another kind of relief in mind at the time. I was shopping with a friend in a department store when I excused myself to go to the rest room. As I walked into the ladies' room, I stopped dead in my tracks when I saw three guys—they looked like teenagers—standing there combing their hair in front of the rest room mirror.

"Oh, excuse me," I exclaimed. I was really shocked and embarrassed. "I must have the wrong room. Excuse me."

"No lady," one of them said as he grabbed my arm. "You're in the ladies' room." He was a blond kid, maybe eighteen, certainly no older. Kind of cute, actually, but I didn't much care for his snotty tone of voice. Besides, he was blocking the door, and I wanted out.

"Then what are you guys doing—?" I was going to finish my question, but why ask the obvious? I began to panic at first, but then I reconsidered. I had heard so much about sex in rest rooms, I figured why not live out this fantasy? If so many people dream about rest room orgies, there must be something to it.

The blond kid was still barring the door, and the other two guys were already feeling up my body. "Okay, you guard the door," I said, pointing to the blond teenager. And then I laid a big wet kiss on the mouth of the guy feeling up my boobs. All of a sudden he looked a little taken aback: like "Hey, chick, you're suppose to get all upset and scream and yell and kick up your heels." The two guys feeling up my body stopped feeling.

"Well, what gives?" I asked. I laughed in their faces. There's nothing that deflates a fellow's rape fantasy more than a complying, aggressive woman. But I didn't care about their fantasies. I wanted a quick orgy while my girlfriend was buying her nylons, and God damn it, I was going to have one.

XAVIERA'S FANTASTIC SEX

"Listen, you two-bit rest room lovers," I said, "I didn't start this little sex scene here. But now that you've gotten me all hot and bothered, don't you think we should see this little orgy through?"

I've had to work off man's pants quickly before, and so within five seconds flat—before the kid knew what hit him—I'd dropped his drawers and stuffed his embarrassed hard-on into my waiting vagina.

"Now guard that door!" I snapped back at the blond kid. "Remember, this *is* the ladies' room, and if you guys get caught in here it's going to look mighty peculiar." I then directed the third guy to start unzipping his own pants because I wanted him to take me up the ass.

"But lady"—he stumbled for words—"but, lady, I've never—"

"Oh, no"—I laughed—"you mean I've got a virgin on my hands?" So what? At that moment I was triumphant about having turned the tables on these would-be rapists. And it was a real turn-on to think about all those proper ladies outside the door when here I was—practically raping two young men in the ladies' room as though I did it every day of my life.

I really hadn't paid much attention to the blond kid guarding the door. By now the two guys flanking me had gotten over their shell shock and were performing like veterans. "Hey, how about me?" cried the blond kid. "When do I get *my* rocks off?"

"Keep your shirt on"—I laughed, bucking my hips back and forth—"and drop your pants. I could use a new sex partner. These two are getting a little boring." Of course, no man likes to hear that he's a sex bore, and to be told that in the toilet is even worse. Now I'd really provoked them! And they wouldn't let me go. I wanted to pull out and give the other kid a treat, but they just wouldn't dislodge themselves. Then I heard a woman pounding on the rest room door.

"Let me in there!" she screamed. "Let me in!"

I guess the reality of the situation frightened my young lovers because they stopped thrusting immediately and began buttoning their trousers. The kid at the door looked scared as hell, but I motioned him not to move. "Hold the door," I whispered. And as I fell to my knees, I unzipped him, blew his penis, and brought him off in a record ten seconds. There's nothing like danger to excite a man.

I got up off the floor and checked my clothes and hair in the mirror. Would anyone know? But then, who would believe it!

"Hey, lady," the blond kid said. "How do we get out of here now?" The woman was still pounding on the door, and it sounded as if she had an army of women behind her.

"That's your problem," I said. "After all, this *is* the ladies' room." And I pushed him aside, opened the door, and about four women came stumbling into the rest room.

"Excuse me," I said, trying to be as demure as possible, "but the door seemed to be stuck." And then I tripped out past their bodies.

I wanted to stay for the fun, but I didn't dare. All in all, I'd have to say that rest room sex isn't quite what certain fantasists have cracked it up to be. It's a bit hectic for my taste. Hell, I didn't even have a good orgasm—but the worst of it was that I *still* had to go to the john!

III. A Role in the Hay

The mad rapist, the subservient slave, the heterosexual transvestite, the disobedient child, the seduced student—these are all characters we may not wish to be in everyday life, yet in the privacy of our own bedrooms with someone we love and trust, such fantasy roles can help enhance our sex.

True, role-playing may lack the spontaneity of enacting your own sex fantasies on the spur of the moment, but remember that creating make-believe people with a friend was something that came very naturally to you as a child. And now you can play doctor without worrying that Mom and Dad will interfere when you get to the physical examination.

Role-playing isn't for everyone, of course, nor is it to be done with just anyone. Be sure you know your partner well so that you don't end up with a ticket to *Psycho* when all you expected was Theater of the Absurd. With a fun-loving partner, however, role-playing can lead to fantastic sex. Role-playing not only makes fantasies come true, but can also add novelty to what may have become rote sexplay with your partner, and it can even help overcome sex problems—sort of what you'd call a benefit performance.

Whether role-playing is for you or not, sit back and enjoy the following performances.

Schoolday Lays

As I've said before, if you fantasize about a sexual act long enough, you will eventually end up performing it—if it's possible to perform, of course—and the same is true of fantasies about people. I remember that when I was a sixteen-year-old virgin, I would sit in my French class gazing at the teacher, just hoping that one day we would be lovers. And today we are!

Brigitte had just graduated from the university when she began teaching French at my secondary school in Amsterdam. When I walked into my first French class, I couldn't believe she was the teacher. She was a Parisian girl who looked so young and fresh, not much older than I. A petite woman of twenty-two with a tiny face, almost hidden in a mass of dark, kinky curls. Perhaps that was one of the reasons I found her so attractive; whereas I was blond and pale, Miss Audran's skin was almost an olive hue. I kept imagining what her pubic patch must be like under the flimsy Parisian dresses she wore.

At sixteen I was still a virgin, and I must say that lesbians frightened me, even though I myself found other girls attractive. Miss Audran, however, was more than merely attractive. I tried to concentrate on her lectures on verb conjugation and pronunciation, but all I wanted to do was fantasize about caressing her tender breasts, or kissing her dark, puckered lips, or having her hold me for a minute or two. Of course, I never imagined that she was actually into other women. Dangling participles, maybe—but not other women.

I suppose that was part of my fantasy: Because Miss Audran was my teacher, she seemed remote and unapproachable. She was also a foreigner, and she was straight—or so I thought. How I used to fantasize about that woman during school! And now she and I act out my fantasy, which goes something like this:

It is near the end of class, and Miss Audran is going over a test paper with us. I've done rather poorly on the test, and so when the bell rings and the other students file out, I stay behind. I want to discuss my problems in French with Miss Audran. She pulls a chair up next to my desk and begins explaining my errors. She seems so genuinely concerned; she even puts her arm around my chair. I keep thinking how nice it would be if she were actually to touch me, to place her hands on my shoulders and squeeze me, embrace me.

Of course, by now I can't even think about my French. Miss Audran asks me some questions, and I can only mumble a few poor replies in very broken French. I want to look into her dark, limpid eyes, but I can't. I'm too ashamed, and so I gaze at her lovely moist mouth, her smooth neck, and her firm breasts. Oh, her breasts! I hadn't noticed before, but now I can see that her nipples are quite erect. Her dress is sheer, and her nipples seem more pointed than before.

"I don't even hear what she's telling me. My attention is on those nipples. How unusual for a schoolteacher not to wear a bra! How much more unusual that her nipples are erect! I began to wonder why they are erect. Is she sexually aroused? Is she thinking about her boyfriend? Oh, I envy him so!

Miss Audran is so close to me now that I can actually feel her body heat. I'm so hot myself that I'm ready to perspire, and my crotch seems to be throbbing. Yes, it *is* throbbing, and I can feel those juices. My God, my panties are wet! Sometimes, when I get very embarrassed or when I can't finish a test in time, I get so nervous that I actually have an orgasm. It just happens, and I don't even have to touch myself.

"Xaviera, are you listening to me?" Miss Audran asks, and she looks annoyed. "What was the answer to this question?" And she points to my corrected test paper. I have no idea what she's talking about. Oh, God, what am I going to do? I want her to like me. I don't want her to think me stupid, but there I am, climaxing in my panties. I'm so nervous and so frightened. I try preventing my orgasm. I hold my legs together tightly, but that only makes it worse. It just floods out of me in one big gush of tingling, embarrassing pleasure. It feels so good; my eyes roll back, and I swoon forward.

I almost hit my head on the desk, but Miss Audran catches me. There I am—experiencing an incredible orgasm with my head nestled in her arms. Miss Audran's arms! I just keep my eyes closed, hoping she will respond. I wait, expecting to be scolded, when I feel her fingers moving up my legs. Miss Audran's fingers on my warm, wet panties—on my clitoris! I can't believe it, I can't—yet I want it so much. I don't open my eyes; I just relax and let her work my vagina into another pulsating orgasm.

How often I used to have this fantasy! And how strange it is that Miss Audran—Brigitte—is now my lover. Sometimes I think fantasizing about her made my wish come true. After all, Brigitte isn't that much older than I am, and she was still living and teaching in Amsterdam when I returned there after leaving Toronto in 1976. Would you believe I met her after all these years at a party given for me by my own mother—of all people!

My mother remembered how much I enjoyed her classes at school. Of course, what Mom didn't know was that I had a mad crush on Brigitte. At the party Brigitte was with a middle-aged man, and I asked one of my old girlfriends, "Is Brigitte Audran married to that guy?"

"Don't be silly." She laughed. "Brigitte's pretty much into girls. Occasionally she makes it with guys, but she prefers women. Definitely!"

When I finally got around to talking with Brigitte, I practically fell over when she told me, "You know, Xaviera, I used to have the biggest crush on you. But I couldn't touch you because of my position at school. I never suspected you were bisexual until I started reading your books. I can't tell you how many times I've fantasized about you, sitting there in my French class."

You could have pushed me over with a feather. My fantasy had come true! I hated leaving my mother's party early, but what could I do? I wanted Brigitte too much. Better yet, she wanted me. I'm usually so aggressive with other girls; if there's a butch role to be taken, I almost always play it. But not with Brigitte. She's actually smaller than I, but I let her dominate me. Our sex is great, and I don't think there's anything wrong with reenacting my old fantasies. In fact, that's half the fun.

You see, when I'm in bed with Brigitte, we fantasize that we're back in that old classroom together. Brigitte will mildly scold me. I close my eyes and let her embrace me. I feel her fingers slowly working their way up my thighs and into my vagina. Brigitte puts all her weight on my body as she works my crotch with her hand. It makes me feel as if I were sixteen again, a virgin and all.

It's a pretty thrilling thought—screwing with your teacher in class. It just oozes of scandal and broken rules and upset principals. Of course, in my fantasy I'm the innocent party being seduced by an older teacher. That's why I'm so passive with Brigitte; in fact, her domination of me in bed is such an integral part of our lovemaking that I hardly consider it a fantasy.

As you've undoubtedly gathered by now, while no one can ever act out all his fantasies, I come about as close to it as anyone around. In fact, I ought to be in *The Guinness Book of World Records* on that account alone—not to mention half a dozen other reasons.

Spank You Very Much!

"I always used to be so afraid when my mother would spank me," Frank was trying to explain. "She wasn't that big a woman. I guess it was more the anticipation than the actual pain. How strange it is that I remember having my first erection after Mother once spanked me."

Not so strange, I'd say. Frank was just one of many men I've known who harbor mild sadomasochistic tendencies, instilled by childhood punishments. Spankings are part of almost everyone's memory of parental punishments, and strange as it may seem, a number of adults remember those slaps on the backside with true fondness. Frank's fondness for spanking, however, is slightly different from most men's. Frank not only liked spanking women, but also liked getting it in return. Actually, his masochism probably wasn't all that peculiar since so many men are simply too inhibited to play the masochistic role in bed. Perhaps Frank was just more honest about his fantasies than most.

Frank was a fairly successful radio and television announcer in Toronto, and we were taping an interview when he began hitting me with all these questions about SM. My interview was supposed to deal with *Xaviera on the Best Part of a Man,* and although there were a few passages on bondage in the book, it was by no means the major concern of my writing. But Frank didn't want to talk about anything else. When I casually mentioned the subject of spankings, Frank began shifting around in his chair as though he were itching. I couldn't understand what the matter was until I noticed his bulging crotch. The man obviously had a good hard-on, and he was trying to hide it from me and the TV camera. His erection told me that I'd hit on his special interest, so I decided to pursue the matter. So what if a few thousand people were watching?

"The strange thing about spankings," I continued, giving him my most seductive voice, "is that so many men want them. I mean, they want to receive them. Unfortunately, these same men, who are just dying to have their bottoms slapped, are afraid to ask their girlfriends to do it. They think it isn't masculine to play the masochist."

I could see that he was practically nodding his approval. And his crotch was bulging more than ever. "Don't these men understand," I continued, "what a real man it takes to surrender to a woman?" Frank practically fell into my lap. Had I really guessed his secret fantasy? I couldn't wait to find out.

We went to a restaurant after the interview for some drinks, and Frank certainly didn't waste any time asking me further questions about spankings. That's the nice thing about being a sex author; people open right up without any qualms.

"About these spankings," Frank said, trying oh-so-hard to be matter-of-fact. "I'm curious. Are there really many men who allow women to slap their buttocks?" He was smoking feverishly by now, and I almost had to laugh at his nervousness.

"Oh, some do," I said. Then I paused and thought, why not lie a little, just to soothe his ego? He was awfully cute, and how many times had I seen him on TV and wondered about his sex life? On television he always seemed to be in control of every situation. Was he a real SM freak at heart? I took another sip of my coke.

"I must be honest with you, Frank. There's nothing I like better than spanking a man's ass—*if* it's a nice tight ass. In fact, I would have to say that most of the men I sleep with like a little slapping around. The last guy I had was a big strapping college football player from the States, and he just loved the palm of my right hand." Actually, I've probably only spanked a couple of dozen men in my life, but why not make Frank feel good? Right?

"Oh, Xaviera, please, can we go to your place?"

Frank just blurted it right out. We hadn't even finished our first drink, and he was asking me to screw— or at least, spank. I took a deep breath, and so did he. Frank was so excited I don't even think *he* knew what he was saying. I was curious, certainly, but I wanted to check out this man's psyche before making any promises. I'm not a real SM freak myself, and sometimes these mild-mannered guys can really throw you a wild curve if you don't know what they're into. If he could be so blunt with me, well . . . why not I with him?

"So you're really into getting spanked, huh?" Frank said nothing; he just looked down at his gin and tonic. "Come on, be honest."

"Well, I suppose so," he said, almost in a whisper, "at least with my former wife, Tina. She really liked it when I would spank her good with my hands. We used to have a lot of little bedroom games. Sometimes she would be the 'naughty girl.' I would scold her like a father for disobeying me. Maybe she really had done something I didn't like—like spending too much money on a dress or swinging with some guy I didn't care for. I would chase her around the house. I'd catch her, and then I'd let her go; it was a fun game, right? Of course, when I caught her for the umpteenth time, I'd bend her over my knee, take down her skirt, and start smacking her ass. God, she had a great ass, too. A plump ass that was perfectly white. Soft and white like two big balls of cotton. I never hit her hard. Just lots of little slaps. Maybe her buttocks would get nice and red and some prickly tingles would run through her body. But Tina liked it.

"Sometimes I'd even finger her clitoris a little between spankings. I'd masturbate her, and then I'd scold her for having an orgasm. And I'd spank her again, as though I were punishing her for enjoying sex. We both got off on that. When we were kids, our parents were very strict about our not having sex. Hell, I was a virgin until I was twenty-five!"

That last comment just kind of slipped out of him. Frank looked embarrassed and quickly took another sip of his drink. He said nothing and simply stared into that gin and tonic.

"Well, it sounds like a pretty good sex life," I said, trying to break the silence. "May I ask why you got a divorce?"

Frank laughed nervously. "You can never really pinpoint why. A number of things, I guess."

"Did she ever spank you?" I asked. Frank gulped on an ice cube.

"No, never!" he shouted, and then he paused, only to begin speaking again, this time in a softer tone. "That was one of the problems. Tina just couldn't bring herself to spank me. She thought it just wasn't manly of me to want something like that. In fact, she laughed at me when I requested it."

Suddenly I felt sorry for Frank. If he wanted to be spanked and paddled and slapped around in the privacy of my bedroom, then why shouldn't I oblige? There's nothing like a rejected man to bring out the mother in me. And a few other things as well.

When we got back to my apartment, I blindfolded Frank. I thought that might help him get over his inhibitions. Frank would be a more willing partner if he didn't know what was coming . . . and going. After all, I had a lot more in store for him than the palm of my hand.

First, I took out a long, narrow two-foot paddle some man back in New York had given me as a birthday present. When the paddle hits your body, it sends a mild tingling sensation through your skin, but it's so designed that its bark is worse than its bite. Mostly, it's just a lot of noise.

While Frank was blindfolded and sitting on the bedroom carpet, I walked around the room, cracking the paddle against my thigh. "Sound good?" I asked. Frank sat there silently, biting his lips. "It'll feel even better than it sounds."

I stripped off his trousers and landed that paddle smack against his buttocks. Frank yelped with pain, but I knew it was mostly psychological. This paddle wouldn't do much more than make a lot of noise and turn his ass a light shade of pink. Of course, Frank never asked me to stop hitting his ass with that noisy paddle. He just kept taking it—like a man.

Masochists like an element of pain, but they also

like the sadist to be comforting. "I'm going to stop now," I told him. "I think you've had enough for one session." And then I held him tightly, as though he were a little child. Masochists love tender, loving care after a sex ordeal, and so I poured some lotion over his pink ass to soothe the tingling sensation my paddle had made. I even poured lotion on my fingers and started working them in his ass. Frank moaned and groaned so much when I entered my finger into his anus that I wondered if I was hurting him. "Does this hurt?" I asked. I really was concerned; he sounded so distressed.

"Oh, no," Frank moaned. "It feels so good. Tina never did that, either." Poor boy, I thought, what else had this woman refused him?

"Wait here," I said, as though he would leave me, and went to my pleasure drawer and pulled out a fake string of pearls. Rubbing the lotion all over them first, I gently began to stuff the pearls up Franks's ass.

"What're you doing?" Frank asked. He sounded frightened, and of course, that really got me going. I didn't tell him, though.

"Just take it easy," I whispered, as I continued my stuffing.

When I got the entire string in, I slowly began to pull them out. Well, Frank practically went crazy. The sensation of those pearls rubbing against his prostrate gland was so incredible that he almost passed out on me.

When I finally took the blindfold from Frank's eyes, I wondered how many other men had missed the sexual release of being a masochist at the mercy of a woman. It's sad, really. Sublime crime and punishment—it's not for women only.

Bound for Glory

Men fake orgasms, too. A surprising number of men can make love for hours but have problems with ejaculation. Not long ago I was seeing a man who could really satisfy me in bed, but unfortunately he often faked his orgasms. What could I do? I tried all my favorite techniques, but nothing seemed to work. Finally, I decided to get at his most secret desire, and so I asked him point-blank, "Joe, what's your most incredible fantasy? What will really make you cream your jeans?"

"Why, going to bed with you, Xaviera," he replied.

Wrong answer! Obviously, I wasn't using the right approach to this man's fantasy life. Joe was too nice and too reserved a guy just to let it all hang out. Then I said, "You know what really gets me hot? I just love to think about having my feet wrapped in cellophane while a big stud of a football player screws me. And while we're doing it, I'm on a busy street corner licking the four-inch clitoris of a lovely lesbian teenager. That's a fantasy that really gets me going."

"Wow!" he said. "I guess my fantasy of being raped by a beautiful woman while I'm tied to a bed isn't so weird after all."

I took a deep breath. Who'd have thought that this successful Wall Street lawyer would ever think about, much less masturbate to such a fantasy? I begged him to describe his fantasy in detail.

"My fantasy begins," he said, "when I'm home alone in bed. I'm reading a book when I hear a strange noise in the living room. The entire apartment is dark, but I go into the next room to see what's the matter. It's dark, too dark to see anything, and so I try to turn on a light. That's when a hand grabs me from behind and I feel a gunlike object jab into my backbone. 'Who is it?' I scream. My hands are up in the air, and I begin to turn around slowly. In the dim light I can just barely make out a form.

" 'Get back into the bedroom!' The voice is high and muffled. Of course, I obey. The lights are on in the bedroom, and when I turn around to look at this fiendish man, the lights go out.

" 'Get in bed,' the crook says. I crawl between the sheets. The moon is full, so there is some light in the room. It looks all grayish blue and eerie. But I can't make out the guy. He doesn't seem that large, but I'm not going to fight him.

"I'm wearing pajamas, silk pajamas in this fantasy. But they don't stay on my body for long. The burglar rips them off me while I'm in bed and starts using the pieces to tie my wrists and ankles to the bedposts. The criminal begins to take off his clothes. I'm crying. God, I've never fucked with a man before, and I don't want to either.

" 'Please don't,' I sob. 'Take anything you want. Just please don't screw me. Please, please don't take me like this. I won't turn you in to the—' Whack! I feel his cold leather glove smack me across the face. The scoundrel, though, doesn't say a word.

"By now he's taking off his clothes. I'm still crying, trying to control myself. I can't. I can't look at him. I just expect the worst. My eyes are closed. Then I feel the criminal getting in bed with me. He straddles my body. I feel his skin against mine. His body weight is hanging over mine. God, I can even feel his pubic hair, his wet pubic hair! Wait . . . wait . . . what's going on here. . . . Jesus, I don't believe this! I feel this body warmth, wet and soft, cover my penis. I'm actually hard in no time at all.

"God, I'm being raped by a *woman*! The criminal is a woman who's taking my cock against my will! She's taking me, using my body for her own pleasures. I look up into her face at last. How beautiful! My erection gets larger. I've never felt this excited before. I hang onto her hips as they bounce up and down against my pelvis. I hang on for dear life. She's so tight at first that my hard-on almost hurts, but gradually she loosens up to each of my thrusts.

" 'Finger my clit,' she commands. I do. It's tiny, though, and I have trouble finding it. Finally, she points to it with her finger, and I run her clitoris between my fingers. Her juices begin to cover my hand. I can smell her feminine juices. She makes me lick my own fingers so that I can taste her insides. She starts to writhe more and more violently as I finger her. Long blond hair. Her long blond hair is hanging down around her face now. I can't make out her face there's so much hair, but her body is beautiful. Nice little tits, firm and soft to the touch. Her hips are much wider but not that wide. She rides me harder and harder until I can't prevent myself from coming.

" 'God, I've gotta come. I've gotta come!' I yell.

"I'm afraid to, though. Will she get angry and pissed off if I climax prematurely? I hold back as long as possible. Finally, I've passed the point of no return. She presses her pelvis down even harder and takes my entire cock up into her wet box. I shoot up into her. It's—well it's fantastic!

"Believe me, Xaviera, I always have my most violent

XAVIERA'S FANTASTIC SEX

orgasms when I fantasize about this lady burglar. Do you think I'll ever be able to act out my fantasy?"

"How about tonight?" I replied.

You may say that my acting out such a fantasy with Joe makes it no longer a fantasy, that it then becomes reality. Not so. We're just playacting. I'm not really a criminal. My gun is a toy pistol. Joe is certainly not being taken by force. The scenario is set beforehand. We're only acting out one man's rape fantasy, with him as the rapee.

The fantasy is Joe's, not mine. Even so, I got off on his little charade of being "raped" by a woman. I actually liked having a big virile man writhe helplessly beneath my excited crotch. His moans of pleasure and frightened delight made me feel so superior and sexy. I guess it's what you call the master-for-a-day syndrome.

Best of all, though, is the fact that Joe really got his rocks off, and I helped him do it. There was no faking an orgasm this time around. He enjoyed himself ecstatically and so did I.

"What can I ever do to thank you, Xaviera?" he asked me.

"You don't have to thank me," I answered. "I enjoyed your fantasy as much as you did. However, if you really want to do something special for me, you know I have fantasies, too, that I'd like to act out."

"What's *your* fantasy? How can I help you realize it?"

"Oh," I replied casually, "it's very simple. All you have to do is find me a teenage lesbian with a four-inch clitoris. I'll do the rest."

This Sporting Life

Richard was the boy who took my virginity. I was seventeen at the time, and we performed the ritual in a friend's apartment. As I've written earlier, it was fantastic sex with no pain and no bleeding. I remained faithful to Richard for a few months after that first time, and although we confessed our love to each other, neither of us was exactly passionate about our fidelity. Perhaps we were simply biding our time until the next lovable person came into our lives. Still, our lovemaking was not without its points of interest to the avid fantasist. We were young, yes, but not without imagination.

Richard was quite the soccer player in secondary school, and more than one girl envied me for dating such a star athlete. When Richard and I first made love, however, he'd been out of school for more than a year, and he really missed those soccer games and the accompanying adulation of his classmates and friends. I suppose it shouldn't have come as a surprise that a degree of this athlete's nostalgia should have entered our sex life. But I was naïve, and role-playing in bed was not yet part of my repertory of sex acts. Or so I thought.

We were in the same friend's apartment about a month after my first time, when Richard more or less by accident, initiated me into the benefits of role-playing. We both were naked, and I'd already crawled into bed.

XAVIERA'S FANTASTIC SEX

Richard was about ready to get in with me when I noticed how distracted he was. I wanted him to hold me tightly and to be passionate with his kisses and caresses. I'd been told so often that a girl can forget about romance once a boy has popped her cherry, and though I'd always thought it couldn't happen to me, there I was. Richard kept looking around the room as though he were bored and looking for something to do. Doing *me* seemed the last thing on his mind. I wanted to please him, but what about my feelings? Where had our love gone? Finally, I had to ask him what the matter was.

"Oh, nothing." He sighed. His attention had wandered from me. So, I thought, Richard has taken my virginity and now he's tired of me.

"Did you see some wool athletic socks around here?" he asked casually. "They were here on the bed."

Wool athletic socks! That's all he could think about at a time like this! I'd lost my virginity and, God damn it, I was ready to taste everything that a man had to offer me—but all Richard could think of were his smelly wool athletic socks.

"Oh, I don't know," I groaned, pulling myself away from his cold, unfeeling body. "I think I threw them somewhere in the corner." I already had one foot out of bed. Do you know how it feels to be washed up at age seventeen? Well, I thought, maybe I'm not a total loss. Maybe I could trap some drunken old man down at the corner pub on his way home to his wife and kids. There must be somebody out there who would still want a seventeen-year-old ex-virgin.

Richard was in the corner, picking up his socks. He was actually putting them on. Was he leaving me already? Where, I wondered, were my clothes? I wanted to get out of that room as fast as possible.

"You might think I'm a little weird," he said, chuckling to himself, "but I really get off on wearing these socks when I make love."

"What?" I gasped. I put my two feet back into bed. "You mean, you mean . . . oh, I was so afraid that maybe—"

"What are you talking about?" He laughed.

I thought for a moment. What the hell is this boy doing wearing socks to bed? Here I was ready for him to lust after my youthful body, and he was thinking about sex and socks? Wasn't I enough to satiate his lust? Yes, I was really put off—but still I felt a strange sexual excitement through my body.

How naïve I was! Richard merely wanted to role-play in bed. I felt part of his excitement but didn't know what to make of it at the time. He liked the idea of being an athlete, but his job as a clerk in a department store wasn't conducive to that fantasy. How honest and open he was in wanting to share his fantasy with me. If those wool athletic socks would help recapture some of that soccer field magic for him—the fans cheering and the girls swooning—then by all means I should have complied. And I did, but it wasn't until much later that I truly understood the philosophy of fantasies.

As I've already stated in my introduction to this book, exchanging fantasies and role-playing with your partner is not a substitute for the real thing. Rather, it's a sign of openness and trust in each other. To participate in a fantasy of his means that you are willing to accept just one more facet of his personality.

That evening I was a little put off at Richard's wearing his socks to bed with me. But that was my mistake, not his. At heart, of course, I was a true fantasist, and after a few more sessions in bed with those socks, I began to love the feel of the heavy wool rubbing up against my calves as we locked loins. Since Richard liked thinking that he still was that hot soccer player stud, I began playing along with him, telling him how big and strong he was. Actually, his fantasy soon became mine, and in no time he really felt bigger and stronger to me.

When I left Amsterdam a few years later, I had had many boyfriends, but occasionally I would still get together with Richard. It was a rare screw that didn't include those wool socks. On our last date together, just a few days before I left the city, I wanted to give him a going-away present. Of course, by that time his wool athletic socks seemed downright tame to me. I thought it would be fun to expand on his role-playing fantasy, so I decided to help complete that soccer-player image and give him something to remember me by.

The evening before my departure we made a round of all the pubs in Amsterdam, and so we were pretty high by the time we got to my apartment. (I was no longer living with my parents; my sex life had seen to that.) "Richard, my present to you is on the kitchen table," I said. "Get it and bring it in here."

While he was in the other room, I quickly threw off my clothes so that I was naked when he returned. Richard was surprised that I had already undressed, but I asked him to leave his clothes on for the moment. "Open your gift first," I whispered. And I pressed my naked body up against his. It always makes a man feel stronger, more in control when you're undressed and he's fully clothed. And I don't mind feeling a little submissive—when it's *my* idea!

I can't describe the look in his eyes when he opened the box and pulled out a pair of red nylon soccer trunks. "Well, what am I supposed to do with these?" He asked. How naïve! I thought. And he was my teacher!

"Give them to me," I said, grabbing them away from him. "See this hole in the crotch?" And I stuck my finger through his crotchless soccer trunks. "Take a guess what's supposed to go through there? After all, aren't you getting a little tired of your wool-socks routine?"

Richard threw off his clothes and dove into those crotchless trunks in record time. Of course, his penis was already hard, and it just popped up right through those trunks. I couldn't wait for him to take me. I wanted to feel that smooth, silky nylon against his ass, to feel it rub against my pelvis with his hard, warm erection in me. I guess Richard wanted the same thing because he didn't even bother with any foreplay; he just took me in one big thrust of his erection. I couldn't believe how much these red nylon soccer trunks improved his rhythm.

His ass fitted tightly against those trunks. I just kept rubbing and rubbing my hands over it until I found my fingernails ripping and tugging away at the material. I don't know what came over me, but in a few minutes his trunks were in shreds. The feel of his hot sweating skin through that nylon and the sound of my tearing his trunks—it just got me going until there was no stopping. That's the nice thing about wearing a bit of clothing to bed; it's such sweet torture to get at the other person's body through all that material. But I wasn't in bed now—not in my mind, at least. No, Richard and I were role-playing, and it was as though he'd finished a soccer game and we were back in the men's locker room. We couldn't wait to get home, so we had to make love right there on the locker-room floor. We were so hot I couldn't wait to take off his trunks.

A couple of years later I received a lovely Christmas card and package from Richard. I was living in New York City, and Richard had married. He wrote the usual holiday greetings, except for his postscript: "Now that I'm married, I guess I shouldn't hold onto these. The wife might not understand." And there in the holiday wrapping paper were those same tattered red nylon soccer trunks. That was going to be some marriage if Richard's wife scared the pants off him!

—So Lewdly Interrupted

Beachboy Bob was one of those dream lovers you only hear about—great technique, beautiful body and a penis that is ever-hard. Also, he just happened to be one of my favorite movie stars back in the early sixties, when Hollywood was making all those California beach-party films. Unfortunately, when the surf films drifted out of Hollywood, so did Bob. His career was definitely on the skids when I met him at the Cannes Film Festival in the spring of 1976. Bob was one of the swingers, along with the porno star Stéphane, at the chalet I was visiting in the mountains near Cannes. When we were introduced, I told him how much I enjoyed those beach-party movies of his.

"Oh, I'm trying to forget those," he groaned. "We made so many of them, and they were all alike. Same plots, same characters, same actors. The only thing they changed were the bikinis on the girls."

I was curious to know what he was doing now, but I was afraid to ask. I always thought that over-the-hill movie stars like Beachboy Bob turned into gigolos, but apparently this wasn't true in his case. Bob started his film career doing porno movies in New York City before some producer spotted him in a swimming pool ad and thought he'd look good on the California beaches. Luckily, Beachboy Bob had made a mint from those movies—the surf, not the skin, flicks—and was now traveling through Europe on his own.

He was still a fine male specimen, unlike so many of those pretty blond boys who look good at eighteen but are faded by the time they hit twenty-five. I couldn't wait to live out my teenage fantasy of bedding down with Beachboy Bob, and since the chalet was filled with nothing but swingers, I knew that my time with Bob would be coming. I would sit back and wait for him to make the first move. And then it happened! The host called everyone to his pool out on the terrace. Everybody stripped on the spot and beelined to the water for a swim.

Seeing Bob naked in the pool with the water streaming over his body was like a movie fantasy come true. When I was a teenager, I used to sit in those darkened movie theaters, gazing at Bob's perfect body, wondering what lay behind those faded, tight-fitting cutoff jeans of his. If only they'd slip off in the water, I used to think, and the camera would catch his male splendor for me to see, to fantasize about. And now, in this pool near Cannes, Beachboy Bob was naked as a jaybird, with no faded, tight-fitting cutoffs to block my eager eyes.

I'd wanted him to make the first move, but I just couldn't wait any longer. I dived into the pool and swam underwater to where he was standing. Gently, I sucked his soft penis into my mouth. I could feel him twitch a little, as though he didn't quite know what was happening, but within seconds he was hard. I kept sucking and sucking, even though I was getting out of breath, until Bob grabbed my head and brought me to the surface. And then he entered me. I mean, Beachboy Bob—the dream lover of all my teenage fantasies—put his erection into my waiting love nest.

Of course, nothing is lighter than intercourse in water, and with all that water slapping against our bodies, I felt absolutely weightless. I felt as though I could have gone on forever. Unfortunately, after about an hour of this, it seemed that Bob's erection could go on forever, too. I was already weary from climaxing over and over again, and the water was beginning to irritate my vagina. I hated to disappoint my matinee idol, but his thrusting was beginning to hurt. I knew he hadn't come yet, but finally, I had to ask him to pull out.

Over the next few days Beachboy Bob and I made it together a number of times. I must confess he was a fabulous lover, but when we were finished screwing, I'd always be left with a dry pussy. Bob never once came during our entire week together—that is, not until our last night in Cannes, under the most unusual circumstances.

Bob was leaving in the morning to catch a plane for Tel Aviv, and he asked me if we could spend our last night together away from the chalet. Both of us were pretty tired of the wild swinging scene there, and he wanted us to be alone. It was impossible to have any privacy at the chalet. It was "share and share alike" with all those swingers.

Bob suggested we go into Cannes for our last evening together and rent one of the best hotel suites in town. Luckily, the film festival was over, and we were able to get a room in the Carlton Hotel. At last *privacy!* Perhaps without other people around Bob wouldn't have any problem reaching an orgasm. He'd given me so much pleasure I certainly wanted him to get his rocks off. After all, I was beginning to feel like the husband who couldn't help his wife achieve orgasm. Was there something wrong with me? I'd certainly never had that kind of problem before. Alone in the hotel suite with him, maybe then I'd know for sure what *his* problem was.

At last we were in bed alone, and no one was around to bother us. We had been going at it for close to an hour; I'd climaxed at least four times, but it was the same old story with Bob. He wasn't even close to coming. He kept running me through every position in the book and believe me, he knew them all. At position No. 112, he entered my vagina from behind, grabbed and lifted my legs so that we were walking around the room—me on my hands in the wheelbarrow position. Oh, there's nothing like the wheelbarrow position to hit the spot. I was experiencing orgasm after orgasm, yet nothing from Bob.

It was then that I practically died of fright. Someone was at the door. Maybe it was some drunk, and he'd just go away. But no, this person had a key, and the key was in the keyhole and the door was opening. And there we were in the wheelbarrow position! I'd never been so lewdly interrupted!

"My God," I shouted, "Bob, put me down. Put me down." It happened. I mean, *it* happened! Just as a French maid came barging through the door, Bob's entire body started trembling as though he were rigged to a vibrator. His penis was still lodged in me, but it started twitching like a lightning rod. His hot penis lengthened and fattened, and then it shot the biggest wad of sperm into me that's ever been disgorged from any male member I've yet taken. Bob screamed so loud and for so long that I truly thought he might be having a heart attack. The maid was so frightened by his yelling that she ran out of the room.

After about ten seconds of wild hysterics Bob fell out of me, landing on the hotel-room floor. "I can't remember coming like that since I was a teenager," he said, trying to catch his breath. "After ten years—no orgasms. Why now when this maid walks in the door?"

I didn't really feel qualified to play the analyst, but I tried telling Bob that his need to be "caught in the act" was probably what brought him off.

"Well, where does that leave me now?" he asked, still lying on the hotel-room floor. "How can I arrange to be caught every time I'm screwing? I'm not going to wait another ten years for some stupid little maid to walk through the door accidentally!"

I thought for a while. I did remember a girlfriend who had the same problem. Basically she was an exhibitionist at heart, and so she'd fantasize that someone would interrupt her sex and catch her in the act. There's also the excitement that comes with the added element of danger. I remember how her boyfriend used to pile up a stack of books near the bed, and when he was ready to come, he would knock the books over and yell, "My God, somebody's coming into the room! What can we do?" It never failed to bring her off.

I suggested to Bob that he recuperate his strength and try another session in bed with me; however, I told him nothing about my girlfriend's fantasy. "Just leave everything to me," I said. "I think a little playacting in bed might do the trick for you." I then asked Bob if he would go into the bathroom while I rearranged the room. With Bob gone, I searched the hotel room for various objects and finally found some books and ashtrays that I piled up on a night table next to the bed.

When Bob came out of the bathroom, his erection was at full attention. Seconds later we were back in bed screwing ourselves silly, and after twenty minutes of wild thrusting I decided it was time for Bob's second big orgasm.

"Bob who is that over there by the window?" I gasped. "Please, let's cover ourselves. Don't let them see us here like this!" Bob looked up. "Oh, Bob, no!" I screamed, throwing the sheets around our naked bodies. "The man is opening the window. He's seen us." And then I knocked over the books and ashtrays.

"Where, Xaviera, where?" Bob cried, and in an instant he was experiencing yet another climactic orgasm. It seemed that Beachboy Bob had become so inured to sex, from all those porno films he had made, that getting caught by a third party was the only way he could make sex exciting.

I told him about my book trick and suggested he try it with other girls in case his problem recurred. Now who said, "Nothing beats a good book in bed"?

Girl Meets Buoy

How lucky I was to have Richard as my first lover. Let's face it, when it comes to role-playing in the bedroom, wool athletic socks is pretty tame stuff, but they're as good a place to begin as any for the amateur fantasist. How different my entire sex life might have been if my second bed partner, a sailor named David, had been my first. I might have been turned off normal sex for good—or rather bad—had I lost my virginity to David. Even after Richard's wool socks I was nowhere near ready for David's heavy bondage scene. But I did enjoy it.

I'd been sleeping with Richard for about six months when I met David. We met at a surprise party his girlfriend Susan was giving me on my eighteenth birthday. If I met David today, with all my experience in judging charter, I probably could have seen from his eyes that he was into sadism.

Since David was a sailor and usually away at sea, I had never met him before even though I knew Susan quite well. I used to tell her all about my lovemaking with Richard—the wool athletic socks, everything. Susan would only laugh. "That's kid stuff, Xaviera. You don't know what a really wild man is until you've tried a sailor."

And then she'd pine away for hours, days, weeks, waiting for her man to come home from the sea. I'm sure that was part of the attraction. After all, how many of us can sustain our sexual enthusiasm when we're in constant contact with the other person? Absence is the mother of imagination. The absent lover is like a piece of blank paper on which you can fill in your fantasies at will.

Well, David, the sailor, was no blank piece of paper, as I was soon to learn. He came with his fantasies already filled in. He had a thoroughly ritualistic concept of lovemaking, and either you conformed to it or he didn't play with you. And I so much wanted David to play with me!

It was a beautiful surprise party, and as luck would have it, Richard couldn't make it. He'd been ill with the flu for some time, and to be honest, I was getting rather horny. Even though I had lost my virginity a mere six months earlier, I was what you might call a "fast learner." I'd waited so long—now I was hot for action.

When I saw David, I could hardly contain myself. Having lived in Amsterdam, I'd always heard so much about sailors. When they were masculine, I'd heard, they were masculine to the hilt. David, with his sailor's crew cut and rugged physique, looked masculine to the hilt all right. There was this handsome blond head sitting on a thick neck, the shoulders of a weight lifter and oversized biceps and torso. Generally, I'm not attracted to that kind of man these days—the iron pumpers can go pump iron as far as I'm concerned—but to an impressionable girl, David seemed my idea of what a stud would be. And I'd never had one of *those* creatures before.

I could fantasize, I thought, but David was Susan's man. He was leaving town the next day, so I might as well forget about him. I'd just have to pray for Richard's speedy recovery. Still, it would be awfully nice to try out a man like David. Once would be enough. My God, I was already eighteen, and I'd had only one man in my entire life!

Later that evening, around midnight, most guests had left the party. I was helping Susan and David clean up when she suggested that her boyfriend drive me home. "It really is late, David, and Xaviera lives way out on the outskirts of town."

I wanted to be the perfect guest and say something like, "Oh, no, the bus is fine," but I couldn't. Just being in the same car with this sailor would give me enough masturbatory fantasies to last me until my nineteenth birthday. How could I even feign resistance?

Soon I was alone with David as he drove me home.

Strange that a sailor should have his automobile. When I asked him about it, he said, "I borrowed it from a friend." Little did I know this automobile was David's own floating sex gymnasium.

"Susan said you're a pretty inexperienced girl." David's voice was so low and gravelly! What experiences he must be able to tell. Tell? Show is better than tell any day. If only. . . .

"Well, I wouldn't say I'm quite all *that* inexperienced," I shyly whispered. My body was shaking with excitement. Oh wonderful—we were only a few blocks from Susan's house, and already we were discussing sex.

"Oh, you've really had a bit of experience? Do you know what these are?" And he pulled out a pair of handcuffs from the glove compartment.

I took a gulp. "Why, where did you get these . . . these handcuffs?" I couldn't disguise the fear in my voice.

"Never mind that. I think they make nice bracelets for a woman. You wouldn't believe how afraid Susan is of my taste in jewelry. It's so silly of her."

I didn't realize where David was taking me, but right now we were heading on the Zuider Zee, going in the opposite direction of my parents' home. This was no shortcut I'd ever heard of!

I was frightened, naturally, yet I wanted to live a little—maybe a lot. I wanted to experience what a knowledgeable, lusty sailor could teach me. If Susan was afraid of such things as handcuffs, I wouldn't be. I'd show David what a courageous, sexy woman I was. He thought I was "inexperienced"? I'd show him.

And so I tried on David's unusual jewelry. The car immediately stopped; David pulled over and parked near a ditch by the road. Soon he was unfolding the front seat so that it resembled a small bed.

"I've never done this before," David whispered as he expertly spread a blanket over the cushions. "You know, I've always been so faithful to Susan, and she just won't have anything to do with bondage."

Bondage? What was that? It must have something to do with these handcuffs around my wrists. Also, since the car seats now resembled something very much like a bed, it looked as if we were going to find ourselves in a horizontal position any moment now.

"Susan is so uptight about the more sophisticated forms of lovemaking," David continued. "I've always had this unfulfilled fantasy of handcuffing a woman. I love the form of the female body so much. I want the woman to be totally passive so I can admire her body, the form of her breasts, the line of her ass. When a woman's handcuffed, then and only then can the man be the total aggressor.

"Well, in my fantasy, I handcuff the woman. She's completely nude, lying there on the bed. Her hands are over her head in the handcuffs, and there I am tying up her ankles. Her body is spread-eagled. She begins to writhe. This woman isn't used to that kind of treatment, and naturally she's afraid. But I wouldn't hurt her. No, I just want to admire her body. But she's writhing around, begging me to let her loose. Her breasts are big and heavy, and I notice that her nipples are pointed and hard. She's excited, and that gets me even hotter.

"Finally, she's so exhausted that she just lies there limp. Her body and her hair are streaming with perspiration and glisten beautifully. I'm standing over her now, admiring her body. I still have my clothes on; it always gets me hot when the girl is naked and I've still got my clothes on. I guess it's kind of a power trip— you're in control that way. She's so unprotected, and you're wearing clothes. And so I whip it out, jump on top of her, and stick it in. It's a tight fit, so tight that maybe I should ease up on her, but I can't. I start pumping as though I may come any second, and the urge is more than I can bear. I come in seconds—and so does she—but we keep right on pumping, on and on."

David paused, looking at me with restless eyes. I took a deep breath. What could I do with these handcuffs on? I had to be his willing slave. If it's inevitable, lie back and enjoy it. "But can we leave my ankles free?" I asked.

David quickly agreed. It was a compromise, true, but he took it well. Of course, I wished he'd have taken his clothes off so I could get a really good look at his big-muscled body. I guess I'd just have to settle for his big erection. Now I'd have something at last to compare to Richard's.

David was unzipping his trousers. My vagina was palpitating in anticipation. My thighs tensed. I could see David's blond curly pubic hair now and the stem of his hard-on. He was having difficulty pulling it out. Oh, I couldn't wait for it to spring to attention. He had his hand around it. It was just about ready to spring up and out of his fly. And when it did, it was, in all its male splendor, a scant five inches of hard male flesh. Five inches! This is the monster I was waiting for, anticipating, watering at the mouth for?

David knelt before me, spreading my legs, and I had to smile to myself. He was so deadly serious, trying so hard to play the me-sadist-you-slave routine. And oh, how I wanted to be some sailor's slave girl, but how could this sailor be my hero-villian? His short penis just didn't fill the bill that my fantasy called for.

Well, somewhere along with my silent schoolgirl smiles and my relatively relaxed attitude, David quickly put some clamps around my ankles. I was so disappointed by what he had to offer—or didn't have to offer—that I hardly noticed him fastening them. Steel around my wrists, steel around my ankles? What was happening to me? Was I some virgin in a seraglio? Bound, helpless, and ready for action—on David's terms?

There were no more smiles now. David's sneak attack frightened me. I was gulping for breath, trying to loosen my shackles, but what good were my frail, weak limbs compared to the strength of steel? My arms and legs were fastened and practically immobile, so all my strength became centered on my torso. In one big thrust of energy I pushed my hips up and forward in an attempt to break loose, only to be met by an even greater thrust of force from David's pelvis. His five hard inches penetrated me in one quick second, just as I was hitting my peak of effort.

I started panting harder and heavier. As I bucked my hips again—harder and higher this time—I began to wonder if I'd made a mistake in calculating the size of his hard-on. For some strange reason, this felt more like ten inches! That was when I first learned you can't judge a man by the length of his penis. My vagina felt snug and filled to the brim as never before with Richard.

My pelvis was still thrashing wildly, but I really wasn't fighting David anymore. I wasn't even fearful now—just excited. The handcuffs and ankle clamps made it difficult for me to move, and that made his lovemaking even more tantalizing. I wanted to hold him, to grab his ass, but I couldn't. Oh, the sweet ecstasy of enforced restraint! Every movement I made had to come from my pelvis. Call it economy of motion, I don't know, but it was worth the confinement, and I let go with everything my eighteen-year-old body had to give.

"That's what I like about bondage," David told me later as he was freeing my body from the bonds. "It concentrates all your sexual energy right where it counts. The action isn't diluted into your feet or your fingertips." And gazing at my crotch, David slowly bent over me and kissed my vagina.

I was only eighteen at the time, yet what a lesson to learn so early. I'd always thought of bondage, if I ever thought of it at all, as some kind of dangerous ritual played between "masters" and their "slaves." Well, I suppose that is part of the fantasy, and there's nothing wrong with that, at least the fantasy part. But whoever would have thought that bondage actually builds pussy power by placing every ounce where it counts?

Is it a fantasy worth trying on for size? That's something every woman has to decide for herself.

IV. Xaviera's Fail-Safe Fantasy Kit

So you're bored with the same old "rape" act on the living-room couch? You don't enjoy sadomasochistic fantasies tied hand and foot with your mother's nylons? Tatoos of snakes in intercourse don't turn you on? Could it be you don't care to fantasize?

No, there's absolutely nothing wrong with your fantasy life. Problem is, you may need to "coattail" someone's wilder imagination, an imagination that takes you beyond the ordinary into the realm of fantasizing the improbable.

Be my guest. This book is full of fantasies of all sizes, sorts, and shapes. Don't hold back—and don't be afraid. What can you lose?

Okay, there's the other side of that coin. What can you gain? A great deal—a supercharged sex life, pleasant recreation for what could otherwise be a boring plane trip or a long, dull wait in somebody's reception room, and a feeling of release from the confinements of convention, not only in the area of sex, but in all your thinking.

Best of all, in a world where even the lustiest of us has sexual frustrations now and then, the realm of fantasy is the one area where you can't possibly fail. After all, you're completely and solely in charge, so you can make the fantasy come out any way your little heart desires.

In other words, what I'm offering you in this book is nothing less than Xaviera's Fail-Safe Sex Fantasy Kit.

The Mouth That Roared

"If I just had another inch." "What would it be like to have a thick nine inches instead of my slender six?" "I'd like nothing better than to make love with a really big instrument, something a tuba player couldn't even get his mouth around."

Many men measure their sexual prowess in terms of how much they give and how much they get. Personally, I prefer quality to quantity, and most women would agree. Yet practically every man I know thinks his sex life would be just a little bit better if he had just a little bit more. I think this penile fantasy stems from trying to keep up with dear old Dad. Little Junior sees his father naked; of course, he can't measure up. Even when Junior matures, he harbors fears that he's never quite equaled Dad's male splendor. And so he creates fantasies about making love and masturbating with some mythical-size organ. This has to be the most common of male sexual fantasies. Also, it's one which you cannot enact. Either you have it or you don't. But please, men, don't let your penile fantasy shortchange you. If you want a larger erection, then try fantasizing that your organ actually is longer and bigger the next time you're in bed with a woman. Just because you are only an average-size man doesn't mean you can't act as though you owned a few more inches. Try putting your mind where your head should be; it can make a world of difference in your performance.

Also, remember that bigger genitals won't automatically make you the best of lovers. Some of these big guys come at me with that hey-look-what-I've-got-for-you-little-girl attitude and think I should be grateful for just getting laid by It. Give me a man with a good mind anytime, a mind that can interact with yours, and a man who isn't afraid to play your farthest-out fantasy games and to share his with you. Didn't Teddy Roosevelt say, "Talk softly and carry a big stick"? Sometimes the talk is more important than the stick—in love as in politics.

Good lovers with small penises usually try to compensate for what they feel they're lacking, and often fantasy is what adds those missing inches. I used to think that the penis was the only male sex organ, and so I liked them big, but Jack taught me differently. What a crazy, wild imagination he had! According to his last count, Jack—a state supreme court judge, of all things—told me that he had at least twenty-eight sex organs on his body! Through fantasy he'd so developed certain sections of his anatomy—like his toes and his fingers, even his nose—that he could experience an orgasm merely by sucking or rubbing that particular part of his body.

I met Jack at a cocktail party given for me shortly before I left Toronto for Europe. One of my neighbors in the apartment building had been dating Jack for just a few weeks, and after they'd had one of their wild weekends in bed, I'd hear all about her multiple orgasms.

"I lost count, Xaviera," Gloria would say. "He's by far the greatest lover I've ever had. Orgasm after orgasm after orgasm..."

Of course, I was eager to learn more about this

man's great technique, but I'd had such bad luck with double-crossing judges back in New York City that I had no desire to meet another man of *that* profession.

"So what makes him such a fabulous lover?" I'd ask, only half believing her multiple orgasm stories. But Gloria would never tell me. I guessed that he had the biggest penis she'd ever taken. But Gloria laughed and denied it. A football player build maybe? Gloria only laughed louder and said, "Xaviera, he's a *judge!*"

Okay, not a superstud. Incredible foreplay technique perhaps? But how far could that get him?

"You'll have to meet him"—Gloria sighed—"and see for yourself. I don't believe in sharing my men, but Jack is such an extraordinary lay that I'll give him to you as a going-away present. After all, you can't be much competition back in Europe."

I was scheduled to leave Toronto on a flight to Amsterdam on the first Tuesday in April 1976, so Gloria's party was planned for that preceding Saturday night. All my Canadian friends were to be invited, and Gloria was to bring her Jack. Even though I hated to say good-bye to all my dear friends and lovers, I must say I was looking forward to meeting Jack to see if he lived up to the fantasies I'd built around him. Gloria had spent so much effort on the advance publicity campaign for this guy that I was hoping not to be disappointed. But of course, I was!

Jack turned out to be a very slight man, with narrow shoulders and really no heft to him. We were practically eyeball to eyeball, and I'm not that tall myself. When we were introduced, he talked in a whisper and was so colorless that I had to pinch myself to stay awake. If he was this meek and boring standing up, what would he be like horizontal? I didn't really want to find out. But Gloria had been so wonderful in having this party that I couldn't refuse his offer when he asked me home. Strange, but on the way to his house I got the feeling that we both were doing this for Gloria. Sex by proxy; only we were the proxies.

When I excused myself to visit his bathroom, I was frantically looking for a way out. But there he was waiting for me in his bedroom. I decided to see it through, but when I got closer to him, I was shocked by what I saw. My heart actually sank. There he was standing before me, nude, and where, oh, where, was his penis? Looking closer I saw something that resembled a penis, but at the very minimum a fellow does need more than an overgrown clitoris. His body looked even smaller naked, like a plucked chicken, but at least it was tight and firm. I was expecting zilch in bed. This chicken would surely lay an egg.

He was gentle, though, in taking off my clothes, letting each article of clothing softly glide against my skin. He even took my blouse and caressed it against his own face. He held it there for a while and then breathed in my perfume. I swear it took him ten minutes to perform this ritual, all the while kissing and hugging and caressing my skin. Gradually I began to feel very, very special, as though this weren't just another lay for him.

I found myself kind of lunging at him, but Jack held me back and got my libido moving at a slower, more relaxed pace. Everything became much gentler. When he caressed my breasts, his fingertips were barely touching my skin—yet it felt like electricity. Shivers ran deep into me. My toes, my fingers, my elbows, my nose—all parts of me were kissed and sucked and fondled as though they were precious to him.

If only he had a larger penis, I thought. But then it happened! I felt this swelling in my vagina, something that was getting larger and fatter. It was a swirling motion I'd never felt from a man's penis before. I looked at my crotch, and there were Jack's tongue and fingers licking my lips, grabbing my thighs, and plunging into my crotch. He kept flicking away at my clitoris until my orgasms were continuous, and then he dug deeply into me with his tongue, filling me more completely than any penis has ever done. Believe me, I'd turn in any man's ten-incher for another session with Jack's educated tongue and fingers.

After our first session of lovemaking I asked him where he learned all those oral tricks. Unlike most judges, Jack proved to be most direct and said straight off, "I used to fantasize about having a bigger and longer erection. I wanted an organ that would really please a woman, something about the width of a fire hydrant and the length of a flagpole—that's what my fantasy developed into. A few years ago I came to the conclusion that I had to make do with the equipment I had. Plastic surgery wasn't the answer; I had looked into that. Cunnilingus seemed the only logical solution."

"But what does cunnilingus have to do with fantasies about bigger erections?" I asked, admiring his talented lips.

"Xaviera," he said, blushing just a little, "I just imagine that my tongue is the fastest, the biggest, the most agile penis in the world. Let's face it. The male sex organ is not exactly the easiest thing in the world to manipulate. It has a mind of its own. My hands and my tongue are a lot more agile, and I can control them completely.

"When I make love to a woman, I stick my tongue between her legs, but in my fantasy it's a ten-incher. To give her the impression of thickness, I fill her with all kinds of thrusts and lots of tiny little licks against her lips. I've learned during anilingus to resist her sphincter muscle, so that I can vibrate my tongue up there and blow in air. Now what penis can do that?

"I've treated women so well with my tongue that many girls have even tried jerking it off. Once or twice I've actually come that way, too. If I think hard enough, my toes and fingers can get pretty turned on, too, if I stick them in a woman's crotch. Elbows are a little bit tougher, but if I fantasize that my elbow is this great big penis, I can sometimes experience an orgasm with it between a girl's breasts. But cunnilingus is the biggest turn-on for me. Some guys say there's nothing in cunnilingus for a man, but my fantasy has taught me that the penis doesn't have to be the only male sex organ."

And then Jack stopped talking. He looked at me kind of bashfully and then whispered, "You know my biggest fantasy? Give me a blow job." And he stuck out his tongue. Oh, that long tongue that had sent so many women—and had sentenced so many defendants. "Well," I thought as I went to work, "here come de judge!"

In Which I Meet a Match for My Snatch

I can remember back when I was living in Amsterdam and a sailor boy told me he wanted the largest penis in the world. "I don't even care if I couldn't screw with it," he'd say. "I'd just like women to admire my huge hard-on. As soon as some chick begins fondling it, my penis would begin to grow and swell. I'd laugh and just watch her eyes practically fall out of their sockets as this little worm grows into a sixteen-inch rod."

I can't imagine that this sailor actually wanted a sixteen-inch erection. It's just an impossible fantasy he'd use to turn himself on when he was alone or when he'd be making love to some girl in a foreign port. But what about those men who *do* have everything—and then some? I receive hundreds of letters from men bragging about their endowments, saying they can't find a woman to handle theirs. Generally I just shrug these letters off as erotic fiction from fantasists trying their best to turn me on. Still, I've often thought that maybe some of those men writing me really do have erections as big as the Ritz.

What does the man-with-everything dream about? Just last year, in Toronto, I met such a man—a teenager, actually—and learned what a problem those king-size erections can be.

Lenny was a young photographer, a student at a local school, who was just getting started in the business. I was lecturing at Lenny's school when I first met him. Whenever I'm speaking in front of a large number of people, I always try to pick out one person to focus my attention on; it prevents me from losing my train of thought. At this particular lecture I remember seeing a cute guy in the front row, taking pictures of me. Since he was using a flash, it was more than a little distracting, yet I found myself always returning to him as a point of focus, and not just because of the flash. He was young, probably not even eighteen. Lots of curly dark hair, fine features, a slim body. A real cute kid.

When I finished speaking, I noticed that he was applauding more frantically than anyone else. Backstage he ran up to me, took even more pictures, and told me how great I was, how he'd bought all my books and couldn't wait for me to lecture at his school again. "Also, Miss Hollander," he began, just blurting out the words, "my name is Lenny, and I'd give anything if you'd model for me. I need a portfolio of photos, and . . . well. . . ." He couldn't find the words, and I couldn't find the words to turn him down.

Photography may be a glamorous business, but it's also a damned hard profession to crack. If I could help the kid out, why not? Besides, who knew what might come of it? I agreed, and about a week later this aspiring photographer and I got together for our first photo session.

Since I've done quite a bit of modeling, I suggested a few special angles and some unusual poses. Naturally, we did some bare shoulder shots. Though my breasts wouldn't show in the photographs, they were exposed for Lenny to see. As soon as I disrobed, I noticed the immediate effect as Lenny's tight trousers began to bulge and then grow and *grow* and *GROOOW!* His face turned crimson as he tried repositioning his pants. He tried photographing me, but with his legs so awkwardly clamped together and that big bulge showing, I couldn't focus my eyes on his instrument—at least not the one on his tripod. He was just enormous. I'm not exaggerating when I say this guy could have used his penis for a knee scratcher. I couldn't keep from smirking, and Lenny was so aroused and so nervous he couldn't handle his camera properly. Between his nervousness and my extreme curiosity I knew we wouldn't accomplish any shooting—camera-wise, that is—until much, much later.

When I unzipped his pants and went for his organ, I grabbed . . . and then I grabbed again. Again, I grabbed! Was there no end to it? Had I finally met a match for my snatch? His equipment was in perfect shape: big, firm bouncing balls; a tremendously long and thick shaft with veins popping out all over it; and a large, red, balloonlike head ready for an explosion.

We were in bed in no time flat. I prepared myself for a blissful descent as I sat over his hips. I guessed that he measured well over a foot; Lenny said, "Fourteen inches at last count." I let out a small cry. Taking a very deep breath, I tried relaxing every muscle in my body as I felt his throbbing mushroomlike head touch my vaginal lips. A shiver swept over my naked body. Slowly I let my lips part for its majesty, when . . . no it couldn't enter. I put my weight against his penis, but no way. I couldn't relax anymore. I was too excited. I pulled off and tried taking his erection into my mouth. No go! Would no orifice accommodate this enormous organ? I moistened his penis with my tongue, licking it up and down in feverish little strokes that made me only hotter and hotter to take him whole—in one quick and maddening thrust. Unfortunately, I had to settle for much less.

With lots of little nibbles around his shaft, by poking my tongue down the eye of his penis and gently biting his mushrooming head, I got Lenny to gush forth with lots of white cum. I told him I'd never seen a penis as large as his. He looked down, blushing. He actually looked embarrassed. When I asked why, Lenny said that while many women admired his endowment, none of them could handle it. He'd only experienced orgasms when a woman would give him a blow job or hand job.

"You mean, you're still a virgin?" I asked in complete disbelief. He nodded yes.

Of course, now I *had* to have him. This would be killing two birds with one snatch, for not only did he have the largest organ I'd ever seen, but it was a virgin one to boot. Two fantasies rolled into one!

Young men have exceptional regenerative power, and so I waited for a few minutes and then began stuffing Lenny's flaccid muscle into my vagina. So warm and so soft, but even in a flaccid state, Lenny was still a tight fit. We kissed for a while as I ground my pelvis around, anticipating any new growth.

"I think I'm getting harder." Sure enough. I could feel his head expand like a balloon filling with air, growing in quick, yet separate surges of power. I could feel my vagina begin stretching. I held onto his hips tightly, trying my best to keep all his shaft in me but, fraction by fraction, though, I saw his pulsating shaft slip out of me. It seemed that I could not take all this boy had to offer. I pressed down harder, grabbing his buttocks, clenching my teeth, doing everything I could to win this battle. Finally, I had to admit my defeat and allow two inches of his penis to remain exposed. Even so, we had a good twelve inches of excitement to share, and we made every inch count.

After Lenny came, he felt so good in me that I continued bucking my hips around. His penis was soon softer but still firm. Those two inches disappeared in me, and it was so nice to take all of him at last—even if he wasn't erect. I came, convulsively, then came again with a wild cry of joy. A few thrusts later, however, his penis began to slowly slip out. When his head emerged, my vagina made a loud popping noise, like a champagne bottle being uncorked. "Happy New Year!" I exclaimed. We both had to laugh; it had been so good. And Lenny was so cute. He even thanked me for deflowering him.

I got to know him better over the next few months, but I could never take more than those first twelve inches. "I've tried stuffing myself into other girls," he once said, "but when they see my large erection, they don't even want to experiment. I guess they're afraid of impalement." He then told me his fantasy about *small* genitals. Lenny would have settled for eight inches. Even ten would do. He said that his penis was everybody's sex fantasy but his own. In Lenny's case, the girl who could accommodate him was always the illuison, and his large penis remained all too real.

"I fantasize," he said, "about being able to mount a girl and insert my penis into her—not soft but hard. We've had gorgeous sex, Xaviera, but even you can't take all of me.

"Remember the Led Zeppelin song 'Every Inch of My Love'? Well, my fantasy is to give some girl every inch of my erection. My friends keep telling me how great it is to freely thrust away with your hard organ. I'd like to withdraw it slowly, let it just all the way out, and then push it back in to the hilt. I've read that it's particularly nice to shove it all the way in when you come. It's just so frustrating like this, knowing that I have to hold back those last two inches. My fantasy is a smaller penis, to be able to make love without holding back. Xaviera, even if my fourteen-inch erection were just two inches shorter. What a difference!"

A most unusual fantasy! He's the only guy I've ever known who'd rather have a foot than a penis. Or put another way, he'd be happy to trade in his cannon for a pistol.

Executive Sweetie

When I first arrived in New York City, I was fascinated with all those tall buildings and skyscrapers. My first impression of the city was from the air, and when the airplane glided down to the ground, I fantasized that all those buildings were the largest phalluses in the world—just standing up and waiting for la Hollander to come to town. In a way, I guess you could say they were.

I used to fantasize about lying on top of those skyscrapers, particularly the pointed ones like the Empire State and the Chrysler Building. Needless to say, I also had some pretty unusual ideas about sex inside those skyscrapers, fantasies that were soon to become real.

The one place in office buildings I as a secretary never used for sexual intercourse was the elevator. It's possible, I imagine, but most elevator rides are so fast and so crowded you'd have to plan an orgy of premature ejaculators to really bring it off. More than the physical improbability of sex in elevators, however, I simply didn't care for these closed moving boxes as a means of transportation, much less as the scene for interoffice intercourse.

When I was working as a secretary at the United Nations, I remember going out for lunch with my friend Sally. She was my vision of the all-American prom queen: blond hair, cute smile, terrific body, and nothing much upstairs. Her bright personality, though, made her a favorite with everyone in the office.

Just out of high school, Sally was kind of the go-for around the office. Leaving for lunch, we'd be giggling and gossiping all the way to the elevators, but just as soon as those doors opened, her mouth would shut. I was about to ask her about this peculiarity one day, when the elevator stopped somewhere between the nineteenth and twentieth floors, and we were stuck there.

Now I've never been fond of elevators—they give me claustrophobia—but I wasn't prepared for Sally's reaction. Her eyes started rolling around as if they were part of some crazy pinball machine registering "tilts" and she fell against the wall of the elevator like a rag doll. As if having the elevator stall wasn't bad enough, Sally's fit made everyone even more paranoid. I tried fanning her face, and somebody else tried lifting her up, but there wasn't much we could do. Luckily, the elevator was repaired and working again in a few minutes. When the doors opened at the lobby, I staggered out, hanging onto Sally.

By the time we got to the street Sally was fine, her old self again, and she started talking about her date for the weekend as though nothing had happened in the elevator.

"Hey, what happened?" I asked, more than a little impatient with her seemingly schizoid personality. "Five minutes ago you were having some kind of a weird fit, and now you're talking about going to *The Graduate* with your boyfriend. What hit you back there anyway?"

"Oh, I'm sorry," she apologized. And then Sally started giggling. "You know, Xaviera, I was really all right. I wasn't having a fit. In fact, I was really rather enjoying myself when the elevator stalled."

"Enjoying yourself?" I couldn't believe it! This girl had practically passed out on the floor. "You had me worried to death. Now what happened?"

"Gee, Xaviera, how can I put it, but . . . but elevators are just a wild fantasy of mine. A year ago they were just a means of getting from one floor to the next. That's before I met an executive from the twenty-fifth floor. I don't even know his name, but I suppose that's part of the fantasy. I'm not at all interested in him except when I spot him in the elevator; then he becomes the most incredible man I've ever seen. We ride the elevator together about once a week, and I get wet every time. I just have this fantasy about elevators and that man."

"Sally, what fantasy are you talking about?" I asked. I was getting more than a little impatient with her nonsense. I mean, could this girl be thinking of the elevator shaft as some big pussy with an elevator thrusting up and down in it all day long? "I thought I'd imagined everything as a sex object, but elevators?"

"No! Not the elevator itself, but doing it *in* the elevator," explained Sally. "I just think it would be a real kick to make love alone with this executive from the twenty-fifth floor in the UN elevator.

"This man saw me one day down at the newsstand. I was buying a paper and waiting for the elevator. I thought he was going to buy a paper, too, when all of a sudden the elevator doors opened. I got on, and he rushed like crazy to get on with me. He'd paid for the paper, but he didn't even wait to pick it up. He just ran in with me. There were a couple of other people with us, and I could just feel his eyes undressing me. I couldn't look at him, though. Then the elevator doors opened, and the other couple walked out. My God, I was alone with this sex-starved executive. He was standing behind me, I kind of gasped for breath—we had ten more floors to go before I had to get off—and I felt his hand run across the back of my dress.

"I thought the elevator doors would never open. When they did, I just ran out. Now that I think back on it, though, I don't even think he touched me. But I knew his eyes were watching me, undressing me. If the elevator had stalled that day the way it just did ten minutes ago, I'm sure we'd have made it right there on the floor. But when's that going to happen again? And when would the two of us be alone?"

"Do you actually want to have sex with him now?" I asked her. I couldn't figure it out.

"It's not all that strange." She laughed. "I was so terrified of that guy. I mean, he was old enough to be my father, gray hair and all. Not my type. I was afraid he'd do something awful—in an elevator of all places! It was just all too kinky, yet I found myself thinking about it, dreaming about it, and fantasizing about it. I keep thinking about how quick and fast and hot our sex would be. We couldn't take our clothes off. He'd probably just be able to unzip his trousers. He'd lift up my skirt and pull down my panties. There wouldn't be time for any fancy foreplay. It would be just a quick thrust while the elevator rushed upward. A few more thrusts into me, and that's about all. If we had an orgasm by the time we reached my floor, we'd be lucky. But that's not the best part of my fantasy. Someday I'd just like to walk into the elevator on the twenty-sixth floor, find that man alone there, the music playing—maybe something Latin. Without a word, he'd have it out and in me. Down, down, down we'd go, the speed making me press down hard on his upthrust cock. When we stopped at the street floor, there'd be that funny flutter you get in your stomach, almost an orgasm itself. We'd straighten our clothes and walk out into the street as though nothing had happened. I wouldn't even look back at the guy."

Sally went back to filing her boss' letters and memos. I thought for a while and decided she had a point about elevators and office building sex. And if nothing else, they sure beat escalators for privacy, to say nothing of Macy's window.

Ride You Now, Esk-you-lator

On second thought, I actually prefer the exhibitionisic possibilities of escalators to the closed quarters of elevators. Private, they're not, but I suppose that's the whole thrill of escalator sex.

Even after Sally described her wild elevator fantasies, I still prefer taking the escalator whenever I can. Because you see all those possible bedmates whisk past you as you ride along, the escalator is a prime catalyst for creating fantasies. While it's not physically impossible to have sex on an escalator—where there's a will there's a lay—it's highly unlikely that you'd reach anything but the next floor. There'd hardly be time to achieve orgasm, and if you did, you'd risk breaking your neck and his cock disembarking from the moving stairs at the moment of climax. What a way to go! Still, one can dream.

New York City must have the most crowded department stores in the world around Christmas time, and there's nothing like the holidays to bring out the libidinous beast in me. When I was a secretary, I spent many lunch hours in stores like Lord & Taylor's and Bloomingdale's simply riding the escalators from one floor to the next. Sometimes I'd stand by one of the escalators and just wait for some gorgeous man to walk onto those moving stairs so I could step in right behind him and be swept away. Of course, he'd be completely oblivious to my presence and my lewd designs, but maybe I'd even touch his leg with my own or, if he was behind me, bump my packages against his crotch. In those crowds what could the poor boy do? You were already jammed in so tightly that your bodies were usually touching anyway.

My fantasy about escalator sex usually involved one mysterious man. I would be shopping in a large department store, checking out the merchandise when my eye would catch this handsome, dark, mysterious young man by the escalator. It seemed he was watching me across the floor, but I couldn't be quite sure and so I slowly walked toward him. Yes, he was definitely looking at me, but no sooner did I begin to smile than he stepped onto the down escalator. Quickly I jumped on behind him. He was wearing a big trench coat, and both his hands were in the pockets. I just kept thinking that I had to get in front of him somehow, open that trench coat, and snuggle my buttocks up against his crotch.

I rode down the first escalator just a couple of steps behind him. When he got off, he turned the corner, glanced up at me and then down at his crotch. I tried to check out what he was looking at, but I couldn't catch it in time. He was already whizzing by me on the next down escalator.

Now I had to have him. And I had to see what was with his crotch. I didn't want to play his games anymore; it was time for business, and I didn't care if we'd have to do it right there in front of all those Christmas shoppers.

I jumped on the next down escalator with him, only now I was riding right beside him. My arm was pressed up against his in the crowd, but I didn't care. I just looked him square in the face. He glanced over at me—what dark, brooding eyes; he looked even better up close with those high cheekbones and his strong chiseled jawline—anyway, he glanced over at me and then back down at his crotch. Slowly he parted his coat and there was a big, shiny erection sticking out! But just for a moment, because he closed his coat immediately. When I glanced back at him, he was staring straight ahead, his face completely expressionless. I gasped for breath. "Xaviera," I thought, "this is it!" The next down escalator you're getting laid. I don't care if this *is* Bloomingdale's department store. Your time has come.

Getting off that escalator, I stepped in front of my trench coat man, watching him all the time. Would he be man enough to perform this most intimate act on an escalator whizzing by dozens of absolute strangers? I could only hope.

On the next down escalator I nuzzled my buttocks up to his trench coat. The coat opened. I felt his erectoin. I lifted my miniskirt and dropped my panties just a little. His erection entered me and . . . good Lord, we were doing it there on Bloomingdale's fourth-floor escalator! I watched the faces on the Christmas shoppers, and no one seemed alarmed; in fact, no one even seemed to notice, but I figured that was because he was covering our private party with his trench coat.

By the time we got to the second-floor escalator I was ready to come, but then I spotted a blond teenager in a high school letter jacket. I guess our lovemaking was getting pretty obvious by then because the kid's eyes seemed to be bugging out of his head. Unfortunately for him, he was taking the second-floor up escalator, but I must say he kept watching us as long as possible.

I couldn't hold myself back, and finally, I had to have my orgasm. I tried to keep it silent, but somehow I was so excited that I just started screaming a high, piercing cry. People immediately stared, looking to see if I was okay, but in my ecstasy I just feigned an embarrassed little smile. "I'm okay," I said with a sigh. "I'm okay." Still, the man would not dislodge his penis from my vagina. I kept hoping he would come. I mean, we were practically running out of escalators, and I didn't know if I'd be able to disguise our intercourse on the store's main floor. Then I felt it. I felt him throb in me. His erection swelled and lengthened and shot its cum into me. No sooner did he climax than he withdrew and ran ahead of me. I saw him running through the crowds on the main floor and out the door to the street. He was gone. And my fantasy was over.

Monosexuality: I'm in Love with a Wonderful Guy—Myself

How many men fantasize about sucking their own penis? Not just gay men, but heterosexuals who want to feel their own organ in their mouth, to taste their own sperm.

A few men I've known have such unusual body structure—and I don't mean double joints—that they can actually self-fellate. This is very unusual, however, unless one is an adept at yoga perhaps, and for most men such a fantasy remains just that—a fantasy. It's a perfectly normal desire, one born out of curiosity rather than actual lust.

I've heard this fantasy come from all kinds of men—in conversations and in the dozens of letters I receive each month. One man, however, stands out as being unusual. Jean was a Parisian cabaret singer whom I met through my girlfriend Brigitte. The two of us were traveling across Europe early this year, and we stopped to visit her family in Paris. Brigitte's mother was a lovely gray-haired woman, very old-guard, who somehow was able to overlook her own attitudes and accept her daughter as a bisexual. I admired her greatly for that and even found myself reacting to her as I would to a mother-in-law.

The old woman was very sweet and very much wanted me to like Paris. "Tonight, let's take Xaviera to the Left Bank," she suggested to Brigitte upon our arrival, and so off we went to explore the city's many cabarets and sidewalk cafés. Brigitte's mother must have been at least eighty, and from her youth she remembered the Left Bank as being very bohemian with lots of starving artists and other picturesque people. Today, of course, this whole section of Paris is very expensive and very *touriste*! But Brigitte's mother still loved it and saw its hotels, cabarets, and sidewalk cafés as they once had been. Listening to her talk as we strolled the narrow, winding streets of the Left Bank, I too was soon caught up in the romantic aura of the past.

"Would you like to see a cabaret show?" Brigitte asked her. Many of them were very risqué, so those were out, but Brigitte remembered one restaurant called La Brasserie, where a talented young friend of hers was singing. "I haven't seen him for so long," she said. "You might even find him very *talented* yourself, Xaviera."

The way she said "talented," I wondered immediately what she meant. Of course, with Brigitte's dear old mother there, I could hardly expect her to go into detail. And so we had our dinner at La Brasserie, but somewhere between the crêpes and the mousse I forgot about this talented young singer friend of Brigitte's. In fact, I was prepared to leave after eating when Brigitte reminded me of Jean. "The show's about to begin," she said, "and you don't want to miss this singer." Her sly grin let me know that I should sit back down and watch the stage.

The lights dimmed and a spotlight appeared, illuminating a postage-stamp stage in front of a tacky beaded curtain. "How Left Bank! How Parisian!" I thought, smiling to myself. But somewhere between my silent giggles I found myself in awe of the supermasculine apparition that stepped before our table on that tiny stage. It was Jean, and he was absolutely gorgeous with his slicked-back black hair and razor-sharp features. I can only describe him as being a young Louis Jourdan, but somehow much bigger and more masculine. His singing voice wasn't really very much—like so many great cabaret singers, his range was narrow—but Jean had such warmth of expression and so much charisma that he actually brought all those schmaltzy Edith Piaf-type songs to life. Coming from his lips, Jacques Brel seemed almost intellectual, and gradually his low, sexy French voice transformed La Brasserie into the past reality of what Paris had been for Brigitte's mother. I almost expected Toulouse-Lautrec to come swinging through those doors any moment.

When he finished his songs, singing many encores, I begged Brigitte to introduce me to Jean. She was excited, too. After all, she hadn't seen him for years, so all three of us filed backstage to meet him. I generally hate to be part of any backstage groupie scene, and Jean certainly had a large and varied following. Parisian women, tourists, gay men, teenagers—you name it, they were there. Without a doubt he was destined to be a big star.

When he finally appeared, I couldn't believe how much sexier he was—if that's possible—offstage than on. His chiseled features seemed almost cruelly beautiful now, and he was wet from performing. With all that sweat running down his face, he looked every bit a man in the skimpy robe he was wearing. I could easily see that his body was taut and firm, but it wasn't as though he were showing himself off at all. In fact, he seemed quite reserved and quite removed from all his fans' adulation. When he saw Brigitte among the dozens of people, his face lit up, and he called out to her. Oh, how lucky could she be, I thought to myself. I had to meet him, but not with all these groupies around.

"I can't talk now," Jean shouted to Brigitte. "Call me here at the theater tomorrow evening, and we'll make plans."

When we left La Brasserie and took Brigitte's mother home, I asked Brigitte if she'd ever made it with Jean. I had a three-way on my mind, and this was my lead-in to her for the next big question. Brigitte just laughed, though, and reprimanded me for even thinking such a thing.

"Why, what's up?" I asked. "It's a perfectly normal question." Unfortunately, Jean was not a perfectly normal answer. No, he wasn't gay—but he wasn't straight either. "Bent" was more like it. From what Brigitte then told me, he hadn't made it with another person—male or female—for at least ten years.

"Unless he's converted," she said, "but I doubt it.

He was a confirmed single when I last talked to him, and I mean *single*."

I begged her to introduce us all over again. I'd gotten letters from monosexuals, but I hadn't actually interviewed one. Who knows? Maybe I could use it in one of my books. (Guess I'm prophetic, since here I am using it in this book.)

We waited for Jean backstage the very next night, and when he appeared I asked him if he'd like to join us for a drink. It was 'way after midnight, so we went to a cozy little café nearby for some wine, *lots* of wine! Now I couldn't come right out and say, "Hey, I hear you're into monosexuality. What's it like?" Instead, I let a few drinks pass and then began telling him some of my wildest sex fantasies. Right in the middle of my story about sex in the confessional in St. Patrick's (not with the bishop, just a nun), he blurted out something about wanting to suck himself off.

"Oh, that's interesting," I chimed in. "Tell us about it."

"Well, I've just always wanted to put my lips around my erection," he began, taking another sip of red wine. "It's always been a fantasy of mine. *Always*. I can't remember not dreaming about it." I poured him some more wine.

"I just think it would be so great to masturbate yourself to this enormous length and then bow your head for a little self-blow job." He was so beautiful that I could well understand his desire.

I asked him if he'd ever tried stretching himself with gymnastics or dance exercises to limber himself up for the feat.

"Oh, yes"—he sighed—"I used to do that, but I'm still about six inches away. Even so, my fantasy isn't just to lick the head of my penis; it's to take my shaft all the way down my throat and feel it tickle my tonsils. I want to feel the sperm hit the walls of my throat. The sensation of feeling your own erection throb in your throat at the moment of orgasm—could anything be more beautiful?

"I fantasize that my lips fit right over the head of my cock. And then I slowly begin to lower my head even farther, taking all of my shaft in one gulp. Then I withdraw, letting my tongue run up the shaft and over the glands. That would be ideal, but even if I could only kiss my pink, mushroomlike head it would be bliss. I'd particularly like to stick my tongue down the hole of the penis to taste the semen."

I wanted to begin asking him questions about his monosexuality, but I had to be careful because I didn't know if he'd shrink back into his closet. I poured him some more wine.

"What about oral sex with others?" I asked. Brigitte glared at me. There was a long pause. Jean said nothing. Had I blown it? He took another sip of his wine and in a whisper said, "You see, I haven't done it with someone else since I was a teenager. I'm thirty-two now. Actually, I haven't had any kind of sexual intercourse—with someone else, that is—since I was about nineteen or twenty.

"I suppose that's another fantasy of mine—being able to make love to myself. I have a pretty long penis, so I can actually stuff a little of it up my anus. Not much, but a little. The problem is when I get hard, it pops back.

"Outside of blowing myself, I'd really like to screw me. It's a fantasy, too. I think about pushing that hard erection of mine right between my legs and having it go up my anus. The head would be a tight fit, so I'd break out some Vaseline—or maybe I'd just wet it down with my own saliva. Finally, it goes in good and easy. I can feel it against my own prostate gland and manipulate it so that my penis thrills me. My erection throbs against the inside of my ass, and I start to move in and out, harder and harder. It's going fast now, and my entire body is vibrating from these wild shocks. I can move it by releasing and clamping my legs together, but just when my hard-on is about to come out, I put it back in again with my hand.

"In my fantasy this goes on for about ten minutes. My penis is red and swollen, so finally, I just hold back my sperm and let it fly in one big spurt. A few seconds later my soft organ plops out. It feels so good! I even like the feeling of my own sperm as it oozes out of me."

He looked at Brigitte and me. It was obvious that Jean had been talking to us in some kind of dream state, and now he was very embarrassed. As if to cover himself, he said, "Well, that's all just a fantasy, of course. I know I'll never be able to make it come true."

Jean looked at me as if he were waiting for a comment. But what can you say to a man in love with himself? All I could do was wish him a lifelong romance.

The Phantom of the Fat Farm

Occasionally there are fantasies that are everyday events for some of us but are impossible for others. Some men actually have big genitals, while others can only dream about possessing them. And of course, what man knows anything about a woman's penile envy? Likewise, a tall, rotund woman may have sex fantasies I've never dreamed of.

Last year I was visiting some friends at a health farm near Munich, Germany, and they introduced me to the resort's owner, Kaye. Now Kaye was a rather large woman—about two hundred and fifty pounds large—and she had a sex fantasy of being carried around a room while a guy made love to her. I'd never performed this act, and really didn't care to, but it seemed a good fantasy. Even for me, though, it would take a pretty strong man to carry me around with his organ lodged up my vagina. And it would be downright impossible for Kaye, unless you used a wheelbarrow—and that wasn't quite the idea.

When I was introduced to Kaye as Xaviera Hollander, she begged me to tell her of any sex episodes I had resembling her fantasy. "There's nothing I'd like to hear more," she pleaded. "Even if I can't do it, I'd love to live my fantasy through your experience."

Now who'd have the heart to turn down a sex-starved woman? So, delving into my creative imagination, I began telling her the tale of "my greatest episode in bed," or should I say, "out of bed"? It's what I call my "Lay at the Races."

"I was unsnapping my blouse," I began, "getting ready for a little sex with Dave, one of my lovers back in Holland. I was so high from the grass we'd smoked that I could hardly manage. Then, all of a sudden, Dave came leaping into the room. He was completely nude, a big, brawny guy with lots of hair."

"Oh, I love body hair on a man," Kaye said with a gasp.

"Yes," I said, "and his big erection was bouncing up and down. It had never looked so big before either." I noticed that Kaye was already beginning to spread her legs. I could also see that her right hand was now resting on her thigh. I continued: "In a low mock tone, like a big stud, Dave said to me, 'I'm going to take you now. Right now, I'm lusting so much for your sexy body that I can't wait.' " At that, Kaye's hand reached under her dress.

"I shrieked with laughter," I said. "I was so high and Dave was so outrageously funny. I was on the bed in convulsions when he grabbed my panties and ripped them off. Thank God, they were just nylon! I shrieked louder—almost out of fear. But it was really fun. Then he lifted me high into the air and sat me right down on his hard organ. I was stunned and completely out of breath, to say the least." I thought hard, trying to think up some great romp around the room. Kaye's hand was already way up her dress, and I didn't want to disappoint her.

"Wrapping my legs around his waist," I continued, "I bucked my hips as he thrust way into me. We were in a standing position. I mean, my legs weren't even touching the floor. I was completely dependent on Dave's strength. If his penis hadn't been lodged up in me, I think I'd have fallen off. It felt so firm and hard inside me.

"Slowly he began walking around the room as I hung on for dear life, loving the feeling that I might fall off at any minute. Of course, his erection helped me stay in place. Then he started to run. I mean, he actually ran around the apartment. Do you know what it's like to have a man's hard eight inches inside you while he's jogging around the room in circles? I couldn't believe it! I was swelling up inside. Was I going to be jiggled to death?"

By now Kaye was on the floor, abandoning herself to her erotic impulses, and so I continued:

"Hanging on for dear life, with my legs wrapped around him, it was all I could do to keep from passing out. Would I ever be able to walk again, make love again?

"Meanwhile, the juices were just trickling out of me. I held onto him tightly, my face pressed up against his. We panted like two whipped dogs. His tongue licked my ear. It sounded like an earthquake. It *felt* like an earthquake, too! And then he jumped. Yes, he actually jumped up and down. His cock started to hit my clitoris head-on—like a hammer—and then he would thrust deeply into me, not just once, but over and over again. His penis just kept hitting my button.

" 'Please, please stop!' I begged Dave, laughing and crying at the same time. 'I can't take it any longer.' Actually I felt numb by then. It seems funny, but at the time I didn't think Dave was ever going to stop. Finally, of course, he had a terrific orgasm, and he stopped."

I looked over at Kaye. Picking herself up off the floor, she rolled her eyes heavenward and moaned, "Oh, that was wonderful! Even in my own fantasy, it was never pictured so beautifully."

When I saw her a week later, she confessed to having masturbated to my story a number of times. If she kept that up, I thought, she might just work off enough calories to be able to live out this fantasy.

Abstinence Makes the "Hard" Grow Fonder

"Rick . . . wait! Just a little bit . . . a tiny bit. Please, not all the way. No, not . . . not that far. Not that. Oh, my God, Rick . . . oh, *Richard*!"

In my fantasies I've repeated that little episode on countless occasions. How many times have I wished I were innocent again? Or, as the Americans say, "sweet sixteen?" Actually, I was a virgin until I was well into my seventeenth year, but I was a virgin-in-vagina only: My hands, mouth, thighs, and breasts were all quite experienced in the art of love.

I feel especially nostalgic for my lost innocence whenever I have a new lover. Of course, there'll never be a first time again, but that's where fantasies come in. Many people I've talked to say that their loss of virginity was either so awkward or so boring that it was downright forgettable. Only later did they learn to appreciate and enjoy sex. If you're one of these, virginity fantasies involving your first time are probably not among your favorites. For me, though, my loss of "innocence" was fabulous, some of the best sex I've ever had.

I guess you could say I lost my virginity over a period of months. I had been dating Richard for about six months. He was a year or two older than I, and like me, rather inexperienced. I had this fetish, though, about keeping my hymen intact, so I wouldn't let Richard make love to me—at least, not all the way. Maybe it was my mother. She kept telling me, "Be good, Xaviera, or else the boys will call you a whore." One thing about my mother—she was always right.

But that didn't prevent me from having sex; I just didn't screw. Richard would massage my clitoris with his tongue or finger while I'd give him a good blow job. A couple of times he even screwed me between the breasts, but never in the vagina. The closest he got was when he'd place his hardened penis on my crotch. I'd feel it flick up and down, twisting against my curly little pubic patch. He'd lower it a little so it would rub ever so gently against my lips. Rushes would run up and down my body as I felt the head of his penis touching my private parts. I suppose that's what makes virginity particularly exciting: Everything is so special, so novel, so intense.

After a few more dates I even let Richard just barely part my vaginal lips so that his penis could rub inside me. He'd rub against my clitoris, and I actually experienced a few orgasms that way. But there I was—still a virgin! Eventually he did put it in all the way. There was no pain, no blood; it was just beautiful lovemaking. We both went clear out of our minds, climaxing together with a great shout of pleasure.

I know many people who say they relive their loss of virginity over and over again with their lovers. I, too, occasionally wish I were innocent again and that I hadn't been the happy hooker, but I never fantasize about Richard and our sex when I'm in bed with someone else. What I do is this: With a new lover I pretend that he's actually taking away my virginity. I fantasize that my hymen is intact and that at any second his penis will penetrate me for the very first time.

The man, however, must be very, very special to me before I dream this impossible fantasy. Paul was just such a man. During my last year and a half in Canada I met and fell in love with Paul, who was working as a free-lance writer in Toronto. He also dealt in antiques in his spare hours. At the time I had to leave Canada and move back to Europe we were living together. Unfortunately, Paul's work was in Toronto, and he knew no foreign languages, so there was no choice but to part. We still communicate through letters and occasional telephone calls, but I truly doubt if we will ever be able to live together again.

Why did I fantasize losing my virginity to Paul? Because I fell in love with him before we actually consummated our relationship with sex. He was first introduced to me by my friend Gloria. She had come to pick me up after a local television show I was taping to promote my book *Xaviera on the Best Part of a Man*. Because this show was going to be aired late in the evening, I was wearing a low-cut gown and lots of makeup, hardly the kind of stuff you'd expect to see on a woman at eleven in the morning. Unfortunately, her friend Paul was waiting for us in the car after the taping. With my evening gown and all that makeup for the television cameras, I looked just what Paul thought I'd look like—Xaviera Hollander, the happy hooker!

He was a very proper and intelligent gentleman, and I could see immediately that he was extremely put off by my clothes and makeup. I tried making jokes about how silly my appearance was. "This won't be aired until the evening," I explained, "and I feel so stupid dressed like this before noon." But his mind seemed made up. There was nothing I could do, and I felt awful about it because Paul was so handsome and tanned-looking in his Hawaiian shirt and sandals. His dark hair was all uncombed, and his unbuttoned shirt showed off a well-built chest. He was as cool and casual as a cucumber, whereas I was dressed to kill with my false eyelashes and painted face. But couldn't he see that I wasn't the happy hooker anymore?

I thought of trying to come on to Paul, but I knew that would only make matters worse. So I just had to put him out of my mind. A week or two later, however, I saw him at a country club in the outskirts of Toronto. I'd just finished playing tennis, and although I was a mess, I was glad that he saw me in a more natural state. We chatted for a few minutes, and then he took off for some laps around the pool.

You can imagine how surprised I was when a month

later he showed up at my apartment door to interview me for a local paper. *The Best Part of a Man* was causing quite a stir in the Toronto area, so some editor at the paper sent Paul over to get the story. I knew someone from the paper would be at my apartment around three in the afternoon; I just had no idea it would be Paul. My chance to create a new impression! We chatted, and I did my damnedest to impress him. Of course, I played down all the stuff about my being a New York City call girl and madam. Paul actually seemed a little nervous talking to me; I suppose he had this idea I was going to seduce him and take him right there on my living-room carpet. The thought entered my head, but I kept my distance and remained aloof. Of course, I wanted him very much. You can imagine how excited I was when he asked me to a screening of a movie he was reviewing for the paper. This date led to others, and we began seeing each other casually for about a month after that. He asked a couple of times if he could spend the night with me, but I refused. I knew this was pushing the matter, but I had become so fascinated with this intelligent, genteel man that I simply wanted to know him before I knew his body.

When I'd crawl into bed alone after one of our beautiful dates, I fantasized what his penis would be like. Would it be large or small? Would he be a tender or rough lover? I masturbated so many times thinking about what our first time in bed together would be like. I'd waited so long it would have to be something special. I suppose it's then that I wished I'd never been the happy hooker, that I could be innocent again. Not because I was ashamed of my past; rather, I wanted Paul to be my first lover, as though I hadn't known any other men before.

Usually I'm quite aggressive in bed, but not my first time with Paul. I wanted to be a virgin, and if I couldn't be one physically, I'd be a virginal in mind and spirit. I invited Paul to my apartment for dinner, and I had decided a good week beforehand that this night would be the evening. I dressed very casually in jeans and sandals, but I made sure everything else in the room and on the table was very romantic: candlelight, soft mood music, good red wine, steaks prepared just right. I wasn't trying to seduce Paul, mind you; he'd already asked me to sleep with him. It was simply time that I expressed myself physically. I loved him already.

We undressed each other slowly. I thought how I didn't want him to take me quickly. All during our foreplay I remember saying to myself that I shouldn't appear too aggressive. At first I didn't even touch his erection. Oh, I wanted to hold and suck it so much, to take it in my hands and feel its hardness—but I didn't. I wanted to wait—and what sweet abstinence it was!

Virgins are always afraid of that first penetrating thrust. Will it hurt? Will there be blood? Will he still love me? I kept asking myself those questions over and over again, as though I were a virgin. When I felt Paul mounting me, I turned myself away from him. He paused momentarily. Then he tried again, and this time I let him glide his erection into me. I even tightened my muscles a little so that I would feel like a virgin to him.

I never shared my virgin fantasy with Paul. I meant to—someday—but I left Canada so quickly that I forgot to tell him. More than any other man I've known and loved, Paul respected me as a fine and loving woman. When I was offered the role of myself in the movie *The Happy Hooker*—the part Lynn Redgrave was eventually to play—Paul was the only person I knew who advised me against it. "But Paul, they're willing to pay me a hundred thousand dollars just to be me," I said. "It's easy money. Who can play me better than me?"

"That's not the point," he kept saying. "You've already played the role of the happy hooker, and now it's time you moved on. Write another book, but don't go back to playing the madam and call girl." He even threatened to leave me if I starred in the film version of my first book. At first I was upset about losing the role, but now, when I look back on all that, I probably love Paul more for his advice not to take that role than for anything else he did for me. Of all my impossible dreams, my fantasy of being a virgin for him is probably my favorite.

Borrowing from Peter to Pay Pauline

I've written and said so much about my own penile envy that many people actually think I'd prefer being a man. Nothing could be farther from the truth. I may fantasize the impossible dream of having my very own penis, but when I'm with a man, it's the last thing on my mind. Penile envy is a fantasy reserved for my lesbian lovemaking. Only when I'm with a woman do I want a penis.

My penile desire was first evident back in secondary school when I had my first lesbian love, Helga, whom I wrote about in my first book. Our lovemaking wasn't much—just some heavy petting and tongue kissing and my knee up her crotch. But oh, how I wished I had a nice big erection to take her virginity with.

What kind of penis would I like? I've said before that I'd want the largest in the world, but if we're going to fantasize, let's get a bit more realistic. After all, my young photographer friend Lenny had enough problems with his monstrosity. No, when I dream about the perfect penis, I immediately think of my lover Paul, back in Toronto.

We lived together for an entire year, and during that time I was occasionally unfaithful to him. Paul, however, was always faithful. Sometimes when I'd make it with some other guy, I'd feel guilty afterward. Paul usually knew about my cheating, and he said it didn't bother him. "If you want to," he'd say, "then you should." But it was silly for me to cheat on him because Paul was a great lover. Even if he had had a nothing penis, I'd have found him exciting. But of course, he didn't. And it is his erection that I often fantasize about when I'm making love to my current girlfriend, Brigitte. I guess that's a pretty kinky fantasy right there—my making love to Brigitte with Paul's sex organ. Perhaps that's what I'd like best, a threeway with the two people I love most in the world.

Often when I'm in bed with Brigitte, I fantasize about Paul's being there with his big, beautiful cock. It's an impossible fantasy, though. While Paul didn't mind my making it with other guys, he strongly disapproved of lesbianism. Even if he were there with us in bed, he'd object to my kissing or even touching Brigitte. Yet I think how beautiful it would be to watch his penis going in and out of my girlfriend's trim little love nest. His veins would pop out all over, making his shaft all rigid and stiff. To watch the reaction on her face as he slid into her! If only it were my penis so I could make love to her myself, to feel the inside of her vagina with that throbbing head of Paul's.

The head on a man's cock is extremely important to me, and Paul had this mushroom head—so big and pink. When I'd squeeze it gently with my fingertips, I could see and feel it deflate. Within seconds, though, it would be big like a child's balloon again.

Many women don't pay much attention to a man's balls, but I couldn't help but notice how big and firm Paul's were. They never sagged. Once he even put his erection and his balls in me at the same time. It was kind of kinky and fun, but I usually preferred making love to him with those balls banging up against my crotch.

The greatest moments in our lovemaking, however, came in those few seconds before Paul climaxed. His body would get a few degrees hotter, and he'd usually start perspiring feverishly. I'd quickly slip my finger up his anus, feel his balls get jumpy, and as he shot his juices into me, I could feel the spasms in his ass. How great it would be to feel those spasms as Paul was climaxing with Brigitte! But this three-way would be impossible. It's my fantasy, something I want so much to happen, yet neither of my lovers would even look at the other one. Paul objects to lesbianism, and since meeting me, Brigitte says she won't have another man as long as we're together. Perhaps that's why I fantasize about having Paul's penis when I'm with Brigitte. If she won't have a three-way, maybe she would settle for just his organ. Isn't life strange? One man's meat is just another person's fantasy.

The Six-Million-Dollar Gland

Some women's penile envy, unlike mine, extends to fantasies of penetrating a man. My current girlfriend, Brigitte, used to live with a big rugby player on whom she'd use a whole set of dildos with great regularity. With me, Brigitte claims absolutely no interest in dildos or penises or even fantasies of such. Men, however, are a completely different story for her.

"Some men think it's because I want to hurt them," commented Brigitte, when I asked her about this shortly after our first meeting. "But I don't think it hurts to be penetrated myself. Why should I think a dildo would hurt some guy? I really have to disagree with Germaine Greer on that point. She said, 'Every man should be fucked in the ass just to feel what it's like to be penetrated.' In my opinion, every man should be penetrated so I'd know what it feels like."

That's where Brigitte's fantasy came in. Even though a dildo can really get the screwee off, it doesn't do much for the screwer.

"I have the psychological satisfaction that my thrusts with the dildo are getting to him," Brigitte said, "but I'd like to feel the inside of his ass with each of those thrusts I'm giving him.

"I'm not speaking sadistically. I'd just like to be in a more active position with a man. I know how to grind my vagina against him, or stroke his penis slowly, or slap my hips against his when we're in intercourse. It's great! But what a fantasy it is to have both a vagina and a penis. To feel your hard meat go slowly into his tight anus. To feel him quiver at that touch of your penis through *your* penis. And not some dildo. To feel your hot blood rush into your flaccid penis, making it hard and firm and ready for entry. With a man, of course, not another chick!

"I once knew this chick who had a four-inch clitoris. She wasn't into girls at all—I tried hard enough—so I asked her if she'd ever screwed a guy with it. She was so outraged that she hasn't spoken to me to this day. What a waste! If I had a clitoris like that, I'd use it. On men, of course!

"But it's a fantasy; it can't happen, so right now I have to content myself with dildos. I used to use big ones on my rugby player, Donny. He weighed over two hundred pounds, and I'm this flimsy ninety-pound weakling. I used to grease up those dildos and give him one after the other. With his butt up in the air, I'd sink that plastic into his ass. His face would contort so, but I knew he loved it.

"Still, I get tired of being the god, just watching that thing slip in and out, the suction of Donny's ass pulling it in and then pushing it out. If only that were my own penis doing him, slipping in and out."

Since that first meeting Brigitte has told me that she sees penises as an instrument for heterosexual intercourse. "A cock doesn't have any place in lesbian love," she keeps saying. Even so, I would still like a cock when I'm with a woman. When I'm with a man, who needs one—except the man?"

The Immaculate Misconception

My lover Paul, the last one I was to live with in Toronto, had been quite the gambler when I met him. Of course, anyone who sets up housekeeping with me has to be something of a gambler at heart, but Paul came pretty close to being a professional. As a free-lance writer he never made a great deal of money even though he had earned a very good reputation in the trade. Fortunately, he knew exactly what he was doing at the blackjack and poker tables. Paul was a familiar face in a number of the illegal gambling clubs around Toronto. He was into real gambling, not the Las Vegas kind, and in a good year it was not unusual for him to earn double the income from his writing fees.

Paul once told me a gambling story that began in a casino but evolved into an incredible wet dream. The two of us had been sleeping together for just a week when Paul moved in with me. Our first night together as lovers began very strangely. I wanted to smother Paul physically with my affection (I forgot to mention that he had a handsome face and his torso was more so). I couldn't hold him tight enough. I couldn't kiss his body enough. Before, I'd been a bit aloof with Paul because I wanted him to respect me. As I wrote in an earlier chapter, Paul had all these misconceptions about my still being the happy hooker. I didn't want to be an easy lay—not for Paul, at least. Now that it was "official," however, I wanted to devour his delicious physique as I had never licked, sucked, and bitten any other man's body. After all, he had moved into my apartment, so he was mine, all mine, and I needed no other men—not for the present, at least. But suddenly it seemed as if it were going to be Paul's turn to hold me at arm's length, for that's exactly what he did.

Once in bed, I lunged for him, but he dodged my advances. What's up? I wondered. But soon it became obvious that he was playing games, like hard-to-get. Well, why not? Paul obviously wanted me; I could tell that by the size of his hard-on. It was pointing right for my crotch. I kept wanting him to take me, but Paul said, "Let's not touch. Let's get so close, yet not touch until it hurts."

And that's exactly what we did. We knelt in front of each other, Paul's penis almost, but not quite, touching my pussy hairs. I could feel Paul's body heat as his hands hovered over my body, but he never touched me. My skin prickled and my crotch grew wet in anticipation. His hard-on actually began dripping a little, he was that hot. "Make me come, baby. Make me come," he kept repeating. I held my breasts out so that my hardened nipples were next to his chest, less than an inch away. I jiggled them and sucked them, hoping that he'd come at the mere sight of my highly excited state. Finally—thank God!—Paul could hold out no longer. He grabbed me, we fell back on the floor, and he entered me immediately. His sperm shot out at his first stroke into my hot box, and I came within seconds.

A few minutes later Paul said, "I'd give anything if you could make me come without touching my body."

I asked him where he'd gotten such an idea, and Paul told me about this fabulous wet dream he'd had. It seemed the dream evolved from a gambling incident that took place shortly before Paul and I first met after my television taping. Paul was playing poker in a local club, the stakes were high, and he was on an incredible winning streak.

"I had about a thousand dollars in front of me," Paul recalled, "when I noticed this fantastically heady and seductive perfume in the air. I wasn't surprised, when I turned my head, to find that the aroma fitted the girl standing behind me. At first I didn't like her peering over my shoulder. Of course, I hid my cards from her view. Still, I couldn't help noticing how beautiful and how young she was. She couldn't have been over nineteen.

"The book says that a fair-skinned blonde isn't supposed to tan very well, but I guess she hadn't read that one. Her waist-length white-blonde hair contrasted so sharply with her tan that even the women around her were eyeing her admiringly. It was the kind of silken, heavy hair that just hangs there and shines.

"Her striking appearance was accentuated by her height. Tall women are often underdeveloped, but I guess she hadn't read that book of rules either.

"What appealed to me most, however, was the angelic innocence of her face. It was similar to Susan Dey, the one who plays Lori on the *Partridge Family*. I had all I could do trying to confine myself to a mere hello."

At this point in Paul's story, I was beginning to get concerned over this young, beautiful blonde. After all, this was our first night at home as lovers, and I didn't want his mind to be on some other woman. If this story had a punch line, I told him, it had better be good and quick.

"Don't worry," he said. "This all happened before we met, remember? Anyway, I played my last hand of poker—take the money and run, as they say—and after a few congratulatory comments from her regarding my large winnings, I thought, What better way to celebrate than with this heaven-sent beauty? Unfortunately, at this point, the heaviest loser at our poker table came over and put his arm around her possessively. He was obviously her husband or her boyfriend. He'd already lost about a thousand bucks to me, and he wasn't about to lose his girl, too.

"I hadn't had a drink all evening, so now I decided to celebrate all by my lonesome. Soon I was dead drunk. I guess the alcohol mixed with my excitement was especially potent because I couldn't even drive home. I had to leave my car in the parking lot and take a cab back. By the time I made it back home I simply ripped off my clothes, flopped into bed, and passed out in a drunken stupor. That's when I had this terrific wet dream.

"Usually my sex dreams are pretty brief. Some chick is lying on the bed, and I start screwing her. Nothing really very much to tell. But that night was different. I dreamed I had invited this beautiful blonde to my apartment—and there she was! In the dream the girl childishly jumped on my bed and lay there in a provocative pose as though to say, 'Do you like what you see?'

"Then she slowly slipped out of her dress. 'Well, I'm yours now,' she said. 'What would you like?' Somehow, within my dream, I got this fantastic idea. What better way to prolong my first orgasm with this child-woman than *not to* touch her? So I told her I wanted her to try to make me come without touching me.

"What a delicious dream. I even offered her a hundred-dollar bonus if she could do it. I've never paid for it before either. Now why would I dream of such a thing?"

I had a few ideas about how a psychiatrist might

comment on that subject, but I let it pass. Why ruin a man's beautiful wet dream?

"I half expected her to nix the idea," Paul continued, "but instead she squealed with delight. I guess I shouldn't have been so surprised. After all, it was my dream.

"Then the 'contest' began. At first she tried slow dancing. I was sitting in the bed propped up by a pillow, and as she moved and undulated around the bed, I couldn't believe how young she was. In fact, now that she was nude, the girl looked well under seventeen. A couple of times she got right on the bed and came as close to me as she could without breaking the rules. Not a day over fifteen, I kept thinking as she pinched and tickled her own nipples.

"The sight of her long blond hair was maddeningly delicious because I knew I could have had her anytime I wanted. In my dream, that is.

"Her eyes were fixed on my erection. She was looking for the first telltale signs, but I was determined to milk the moment for all it was worth. I wouldn't allow myself to come—not yet.

"Phase Two of this dream began when the girl took a bottle of baby oil and teasingly let it run down her body. In no time her neck, back, and shoulders were covered with the stuff, and she writhed like a glistening snake in the candlelight.

"In her intensity to turn me on, she began caressing herself more and more. The oil made it easy for the girl to insert her fingers into her vagina. She kept fingering herself with increasing speed, reaching a feverish pace.

"She could just barely touch her nipple with her tongue. Then she began to caress her body lovingly. The sounds of her oily hands squishing all over oily buttocks and breasts just about did the trick then and there. Her face took on a kind of ecstatic look, too. Her goal was to make *me* come, but it was difficult to tell who was getting turned on faster.

"Finally, she squatted down over my penis so that it was sticking up just a fraction from her blond pussy hairs. It was so close that I could feel the heat, and within seconds I was shooting my cum, hitting her vaginal lips as she writhed around in an orgasm of her own. Then I woke up and found myself awash in a pool of cum. I had a wet dream all right—and for real.

"After I awoke, I was still hot and itching for another orgasm. I went into the bathroom and broke out a bottle of oil. When I was covered, I stood in the dark room and pretended that I was holding my dream girl. I pretended that my hands were the tight lips of her vagina and that finally, I was able to touch her, to let our bodies slide together in the darkness. . . .

"So now you understand. I just thought it might be exciting to try out my wet dream in real life. After all, you don't mind being my dream girl, do you, Xaviera?"

Of course, I didn't mind. In fact, I rather fancied Paul's unusual, no-touch fantasy. How did we do? Well, we batted .500. Sometimes he would come without touching, and sometimes I would. One of these days, if Paul and I get together again, we'll make the fantasy come all the way true. One thing I can tell you—it was terribly tantalizing just making the attempt. You ought to try it yourself sometime.

V. Who's Afraid of the Big Bad Fetish?

Fetishists are probably the most accomplished fantasists of all. Who else could endow mundane, commonplace materials, such as feathers, cellophane, or leather, with all the sexual charge of one's own genitals in heat? For some fetishists, the very breeze running through their hair becomes an erotic experience. Silk against their skin causes nipples to harden and stand at attention. And old shoes hold undreamed-of possibilities.

But as with most inventive and creative people, it hasn't been easy for fetishists. They're a much maligned breed of fantasists. Many critics have seen their attraction to various objects as a kind of fixation that supplants normal sexual intercourse. In *Everything You Always Wanted to Know About Sex,* Dr. David Reuben categorized fetishes as anything one enjoys more than penile-vaginal contact. I remember my gay photographer friend Danny, who, upon reading Dr. Reuben's book, said, "My God, Xaviera, I'm just one big fetish!"

I think Dr. Reuben's definition needs a little work. As a professional fantasist, I'd define a fetish as any attraction to an inanimate object that creates a sexual reaction in a man or woman. Far from supplanting lovemaking, fetishes usually enhance it, whether it's masturbation, oral sex, or even "the real thing."

For avid fetishists, too much of a good thing is never enough. Try one fetish sometime, and you'll know what they're talking about: "Feeling is believing."

From Dry Goods to Wet Dreams

One of the kinkiest, yet commonest of fetishes is the desire to handle someone else's underwear. So popular is this fetish that Tennessee Williams immortalized it in his great play *Night of the Iguana,* in which a virgin spinster tells of giving her used panties to a hapless suitor. The spinster calls it one of her greatest "sexual encounters." Such a fetish is what you might call sex by proxy for those too timid to handle a woman on a firsthand basis.

So obsessive are some men's underwear fetishes that I've known them actually to steal women's bras, nylons, and panties from clotheslines. For the most part, these men don't want to wear the female undergarments, although there are those who do. Rather, the fetishist just wants to feel and handle an article of clothing that has touched a woman's genitals or some other part of her body that happens to hold particular erotic significance to him.

Foot fetishists, for example, couldn't care less about a girl's panties. I remember one girlfriend of mine in New York City who actually helped her foot-fetishist lover in his adventures. The two of them, Denise and Charles, used to walk through Central Park, and when Charles spotted a woman whose feet he happened to like, Denise would run over to the woman and say, "My dear, what fabulous shoes. Where did you get them? I'd love to buy a pair just like them. Why, they're just so pretty!"

All the while this was happening, Charles would be checking out the woman's feet. Often Denise could get the woman to take off one of the shoes; that way Charles got a look at yet another "naked" foot, and sometimes the woman would even let him handle the shoe.

"Just checking the label," Charles would say. It was his way of satiating his fetish for women's shoes and feet. Charles wouldn't have cared to wear the shoes, even if he could have got them on. He just liked the sensation of knowing that a woman's lovely foot had at one time "penetrated the shoe," as he put it.

Peter is a different type of fetishist. He loved wearing a certain pair of unusual panties I'd once worn. Peter is my Dutch friend who was furtively seduced by the American photographer Danny.

I remember taking Peter to his first orgy. He was so straight then that he wouldn't even take off his clothes. As Scarlett O'Hara once told prim-and-proper Melanie, "I'm glad I'm not so modest." Yes, Peter was *that* bashful. But since we were at an orgy and I was the hostess, I was insistent that Peter have a ball balling.

"I've got to wear something," Peter kept saying. "I just can't expose myself to complete strangers."

"But this is an orgy," I tried to explain. "Everybody else is nude. You'll stick out if you don't undress." (Either way, of course, Peter would stick out. He had one of the largest penises I'd ever seen—or experienced.)

But I couldn't persuade Peter to undress. At first I thought he could just stick his penis through the fly of his underwear and screw me that way. But he wasn't wearing any underwear. And his thick corduroy trousers were a bit bulky for comfortable intercourse. I then thought of giving Peter some of my underwear, but none of my nylon or silk panties would fit him. Then I remembered a pair of pink rubber panties I had upstairs in a drawer. I had used them as part of my costume for a New Year's Eve party. Since they were rubber, the panties would fit anybody, even a big man like Peter, and they were crotchless, too. He could just slip them on, stick his cock through the gap, and we'd both be satisfied: Peter would be wearing *some* clothing, and I'd be getting laid.

I quickly ran upstairs, dug out the rubber panties, and hurried back down to Peter with my solution in hand. "All right, this underwear is the perfect fashion for an orgy. Step into these. No one's worn them since I dressed up as the New Year's Baby six months ago."

Peter's eyes lit up. "You actually wore these?" He gasped silently, and his hands lovingly stroked the rubber panties.

"Don't waste time. Get them on." I was unusually horny, even for me. Peter obeyed me as though his sex life depended on it. (Mine did!)

Well, the change that came over Peter was astounding. No sooner did he put on the pink rubber panties than his cock grew even bigger—and rock hard. It stuck right out through the hole in the crotch, and he did absolutely nothing to hide his big, thick hard-on from any of my other horny, naked guests. Peter so loved the feel of the rubber and was so turned on by the fact that I'd once worn the panties, that he turned into a hard-core exhibitionist. Peter wouldn't stop parading his hard cock all around the living room and through the bedrooms. I was almost afraid we'd never have sex, but finally, we did, of course. Yet never for a moment, during the entire five-hour orgy, did he take off the rubber crotchless panties. When Peter finally left the next morning, I gave him the panties as a door prize for being "the most active novice orgiast."

I've also known my share of underwear fetishists, but even so, I suppose nothing could have prepared me for the troop of underwear crazies who invaded my Toronto house and home for ten straight days in April 1976. Certainly the announcement in the Toronto newspaper ad I ran was simple enough:

> Xaviera Hollander is leaving Canada and selling all her clothing and furniture.

And then I gave my address and telephone number. But what freaks responded to that ad! For ten whole days more than five hundred people came tramping through my two-bedroom apartment, looking for any bits and scraps of my personal possessions to call their own.

Now, it didn't surprise me that a prominent member of the Toronto police department bought my king-size bed. I wasn't shocked when a member of the city's vice squad paid me twice the original price for my three-year-old black satin sheets. I didn't dwell on the mysteries of why women would arrive with their husbands to buy my sexy nightgowns, whispering to me, "Maybe if I wear your nightgowns, he'll start treating me like Xaviera Hollander in bed." And of course, I wasn't dismayed when a lesbian couple bought my eternally horny gerbils and said, "We'll name their children after you, Xaviera." These incidents neither surprised nor alarmed me. After all, don't most people dream of living the lives of celebrities?

What baffled me were the fetishists who kept begging me for some of my *used* underwear. I hadn't planned on selling any of *that* stuff. I was just going to throw those out or give them to my maid. Throw them away? How stupid of me! Little did I know that a virtual gold mine lay in my bedroom drawers. No sooner did my newspaper ad appear than I began receiving early-morning calls from people desperate to buy my worn panties and bras.

"Worn," they would stress, "and *please* don't bother to wash them." By the hour, my prices began to double and then to quadruple. Men and women alike were begging me to cut my undies in half, in quarters, to bring down the sky-high prices. "Even people of modest means deserve to own your panties," one man told me.

Autographed underwear was particularly popular. "Your name across the crotch, please," they would ask.

I got one call at three in the morning from a traveling salesman named Sam. "Do you have any rubberware to sell, such as boots, dresses, or aprons? Even kitchen gloves would do."

"I'm sorry," I said. "All I have are some old worn, muddy black rubber boots. Believe me, I don't know why I didn't throw them out months ago. They're no good to anyone, they're so old."

"*Old*, did you say?" I could hear gasping and ecstatic moaning over the phone. "Please don't sell them until I get there. I'll offer you fifty dollars if they're really old. In fact, I'll give you one hundred dollars if you let me lick the boots while you're wearing them."

In just ten days I made well over fourteen thousand dollars selling odds and ends of my personal belongings. For the most part these buyers were not interested in really valuable items like my color television set or my stereo system. Those impersonal items went for bargain prices. But give them some piece of cloth that had touched my famous body, and those fetishists couldn't pay enough. Ah, what price stardom!

Spastic over Plastic

Peter, my free-lance photographer friend, is such a shy guy, so shy he never has confessed to me his brief affair with Danny that I described in an earlier chapter. Peter's even embarrassed about possessing one of the largest male members I've ever seen on a man. When he telephoned me one day for a movie date, I said to him, "Peter, I'm doing a new book on sex fantasies, and I need some good male inspiration. Do you have any kinky fantasies or fetishes I can write about?" I frankly didn't expect much out of Peter. No man I've known has been more secretive about his sex life than my bashful friend. But as the saying goes, silent water runs deep, and Peter turned out to be a veritable Mississippi River of sexual creativity. Some might say "perverse," but I prefer the term "sexually creative." After all, why prejudice yourself against a man just because he has an imagination?

"Well, I don't know if you'd consider this a fetish or a fantasy," Peter began, barely speaking above a whisper, "but I love sticking my fingers through tightly stretched cellophane. Come to think of it, it's a fetish that developed into a fantasy."

Tightly stretched cellophane, I thought. This has got to be something, and so I switched on my telephone tape recorder. "Yes, Peter, what about sticking your finger through tightly stretched cellophane?" I wanted to ask him why a finger and not his penis, but one interruption, and I might never learn the sexual ecstasy of tightly stretched cellophane.

"Well, I enjoy feeling my fingers run across the smooth, thin, slippery surface," he said hesitantly. "Gradually it begins to give and stretch. You put more pressure on your finger, and slowly you stretch the cellophane into the shape of your finger.

"When you've just about broken all the way through, but not quite, the cellophane resembles something like a prophylactic around your finger. You stretch the plastic more and more until your finger pops through. It feels so good. I don't know why really, but it's enough to make me hard.

"When I was a kid, I used to drop into grocery stores and stick my finger through the cellophane wrappings on fruits and vegetables. My favorite packages were the tomatoes wrapped in cellophane. I'd press my finger through the cellophane right into the mushy flesh of the ripe, red tomatoes. I'd sometimes stand there for a few seconds pulling my finger in and out of that tomato. It felt so good breaking through the plastic and into the skin of the tomato. The cellophane would kind of pop, and then you would hear the tomato slurp around as you stuck your finger into it. I guess I also got off on the danger of doing this in a crowded grocery store. I can never remember actually buying the tomatoes, taking them home, and trying this out in private. That wouldn't be exciting. The idea that

I might get caught doing something so kinky in a crowded grocery store was enough to make me go hard in my pants.

"After I started screwing chicks, I stopped going into grocery stores and manhandling the merchandise. Still, I had this thing about cellophane. Gradually I developed this fantasy. I spent many nights lying in bed, staring at the ceiling, thinking about going into a grocery store and performing my sex dream. Only in the fantasy I don't use my finger; I use my cock to poke through the cellophane. Of course, I never have done this. You know me, Xaviera. Getting caught with your finger in a tomato is one thing; your tool is a whole different story.

"In my fantasy, though, I walk into the grocery store, holding a big shopping bag. I use the bag to disguise what I'm going to do with my pecker. I walk through all the aisles, eyeing all the women up and down until I've got a good, healthy hard-on. Then I walk up to the vegetable stand, carefully unzip my pants, and pop out my pecker. With the bag in front of me, I slowly press the head of my hard-on against a cellophane package of tomatoes. I press harder and harder until I feel the cellophane give way. The cellophane hasn't broken yet, but it's all stretched out. In fact, the cellophane is now like a thin coating of plastic around my erection. Finally, I break through, pushing my pecker right into the tomato. It practically breaks the tomato apart, but not quite. It feels so good and squishy.

"Naurally, there are all these women in the store who are walking around, inspecting the fruit and vegetables. Even so, I keep on pushing my hard-on in and out of that plastic-wrapped tomato. I'm about ready to squirt my juices when I notice a teenage girl feeling up the pears and apples. I try acting nonchalant, and so I start to check out the pears, too. My hard-on, though, is still in the tomato.

"I begin to notice that she has really nice boobs, and I think I even spot some pubic hair sneaking out of her short shorts. They're *really* cut short, so brief that some of her ass is definitely showing. Yes, indeed, there's a little pussy hair down there too. If only I could get a better look. Of course, I can't with my hard-on where it is. God, this gets me even hotter, so hot that I'm practically coming in this tomato. I'm trying to control it, but I can't, and I just let it go, shooting my entire load. I close my mouth so that not even a peep emerges, which is difficult because my orgasms usually wake up the neighborhood. But I keep my mouth shut. Unfortunately, my body quakes so much that my cock plops out of the tomato and the girl spots it among the vegetables she's squeezing.

"The girl turns so white I'm afraid she may faint on me. Sure enough, she does—and a thrill goes through me as I study her lying there on the floor. Not only her pussy hairs but a part of her vagina are showing at the crotch of her shorts—just like Linda Lovelace in *Deep Throat*—and of course, I get hard again. I won't even have to take her clothes off. Just push a little material aside, and I can enter her then and there, like a tomato wrapped in cellophane.

"No one sees us yet. I think of screwing her on the floor; then I decide it will be better standing up. I lift her up into a standing position so that our crotches meet. My erection is still sticking out, and I just rub it against her crotch until it slides into her vagina. I want it to look as if I'm helping the girl, since several women have noticed that she's fainted. I tell them the girl is my cousin, and I must get her out of the store. I'm hopping along, reassuring the clerks and shoppers that I have everything under control. All the while my hard-on is up her pussy. I come again just as I'm explaining the situation to the store manager. Eventually I get her out on the street, the girl comes to and *comes*, too—and I quickly kiss her and run away.

"It's a great fantasy. Of course, I could never realize it, and I'd only be arrested if I tried. But that's all right with me. Real life could never quite match my imagination."

Peter had a point there, I thought, as I hung up the phone. How could he ever enact that fantasy? Finding a package of plastic-wrapped tomatoes would be easy. But that girl—she'd really have to be *some* tomato herself!

The Night I Got My Nest Feathered

She is still one of Hollywood's biggest stars, even though weight problems have somewhat diminished her box-office draw. He is a New York clothes designer, who, shortly after they first met, became her favorite—lover, that is. Sara Star wouldn't totally give up her Halstons for this younger designer's wraps. Still, with Sara occasionally wearing one of Doug Designer's outfits to an opening or even an ordinary lunch date at the Plaza Hotel, the young designer's reputation was soon enhanced.

Feathers were Doug's trademark, and those gowns he designed for Sara—the ones she would deign to wear—inevitably featured a feathery motif. From my

New York City days, I'd known that Sara was one of Hollywood's swingingest personalities. I'd never heard of Doug until the newspaper columnists began covering their romance. But not until I met Doug Designer at his small couture party in Paris, did I learn of Sara's insatiable fetish.

I was attending Doug's party with Brigitte, and I was admiring one of his evening gowns, which was laced with tiny black feathers around the neckline. Doug walked over to where I was standing and asked me if I cared to see some of his other creations with feathers. "Strangely enough," he said, "I don't have many of my 'feather gowns' with me this trip. They're my favorites, though." And at that he began fondling the feather-laced neckline of the gown I was admiring. Doug said he recognized me from the covers of my books. I must confess that I was not immediately attracted to Doug. He was a bit short and slim for my taste, but when he asked me to dinner that evening, I couldn't refuse. To me Doug was a star-by-association, and I couldn't help being impressed. Perhaps that was my sex fantasy: to make love to the lover of Sara Star. She was a voluptuous, zaftig woman with raven-black hair, and I'd often wanted to meet her at some swinger's party. She'd be there, I imagined, wearing one of those large, colorful caftans that would partially disguise her overweight but still voluptuous body. Laying Sara would be like laying a big, beautiful pillow— all sweetness and marshmallow softness. Well, if I couldn't have Sara, I'd have to settle for Doug. At least I might be able to learn what Sara's sex scene was like.

At first Brigitte was jealous as hell, not because I was screwing around on her but because I'd be getting to Doug Designer, Sara Star's old boyfriend. "I'd give anything to climb into that woman's tent." Brigitte sighed. "I want a detailed account when you get home tonight."

"What makes you think I'm interested in sleeping with Doug?" I said, trying my best to play prim-and-proper. But the leer on my face was unmistakable, and if anyone knew when I was horny and up to something, it was Brigitte.

"Oh, come off it, Xaviera," she said.

"I can't lie to you, Brigitte. Believe me, dear, I promise to be faithful to you—next month. Right now I can't pass up an opportunity like this. I've always heard about those wild, swinging group sex scenes Sara used to throw in Hollywood, New York, and London. Somehow I never was invited. Maybe I was just out of town, but believe me, I can't pass up an opportunity like this. Who knows, maybe I'll even find this designer friend of Sara's attractive."

Certainly, it was one evening I was not to forget soon. The chauffeured limousine to LaSerre's for dinner, *Samson et Dalila* at the gorgeous Paris Opéra house, some coffee afterward along the Left Bank, and then on to Doug's flat on the Champs-Élysées. It wasn't a very large apartment; his main digs were in New York and Los Angeles. As Doug put it, this Paris place was just "my closet for the odd night when I'm passing through town."

To tell the truth, I didn't much care what the apartment looked like. I was more interested in learning about Sara Star's sex scene and, of course, what Doug himself had to offer in the way of sexual adventure.

Well, Doug was right about the apartment: It *was* small. But by no stretch of the imagination would I ever have expected so little to contain so much. True, the place wasn't much in the way of furnishings. The kitchen was a closet and the living room didn't contain much more than a few director's chairs in iron and leather. But the bedroom! Oh, the bedroom. The room was ceiling-to-floor mirrors. That was pleasantly kinky, I thought. Why not enjoy a little voyeurism with your exhibitionism? It looked like a scene I could get into. I sat down on the king-size oval bed and looked up to a mirrored ceiling. My God, my reflection was running off into infinity. This would be like attending an orgy with just two people present!

But that was the tamer side of Doug's bedroom. I was sitting on his bed, and what seemed to be a heavy fur bedspread was actually a finely woven mesh of tiny, black-dyed ostrich feathers. Now I'd worn boas made of ostrich feathers and had dresses lined in them, but I'd never seen so many of those tiny, fingerlike feathers together in one place. Instinctively, I lay back on the sheet of feathers and spread out my fingers. Soon I felt as though I were engulfed in those tickling, teasing pieces of fluff. I caressed my own face in them and felt the feathers run around my bare ankles. I kicked off my shoes and burrowed my toes into them.

Doug was watching and laughing. I guess I was making a spectacle of myself, writhing around in all those feathers, tickling myself and letting myself be tickled. What the hell were all these feathers for, anyway, if not to tickle one's feather fetish? Funny, I didn't even know I had one. But there I was, continuing to undulate in the ostrich feathers even though Doug was laughing at me.

"So you like my feather bed?" Doug asked, amused but far from disinterested. He looked almost sadistic, standing over me with his legs spread wide and his crotch bulging. I stopped writhing in the feathers for a moment and looked up at him. Slowly he began to unzip his pants. He wasn't wearing underwear, and within a flash, his cock shot out at me. With one hand he started jerking himself off, and with the other he slowly tore the trousers off his hot loins. I was so fixated on the sight of Doug pounding his meat that I didn't even think to take off my clothes. Of course, my shoes were already off and on the floor, and I continued running my feet through the ostrich feathers.

By the bed was a bouquet of flowers. When I took a second look, though, I realized that the flowers were artificial. In fact, they were made of feathers. Obviously, this designer had a real thing about feathers, and feathers meant tickling. I grabbed one of the red feather roses from the bouquet, and while I was still lying on the bed, I began to dangle it out in front of me. Soon Doug stopped massaging his penis. His erection stood straight out, just inches away from the red feather rose. Slowly Doug began inching closer and closer to me so that his penis was soon nose to nose, so to speak, with my red feather rose. I shook the rose, brushing it ever so gently against Doug's erection. Doug giggled a little, and I could tell my rose was having an effect as his cock bounced up and down on its very own initiative.

I started shaking the rose faster and faster, and Doug's erection began bouncing faster and faster until I was afraid he might shoot off into my red feather rose. Just when I was about to stop, Doug grabbed the rose and threw it over his shoulder. In a flash, he jumped right on top of me, threw my dress up and sank his thick, hard penis into me. Luckily, I wasn't wearing any underwear, so it was an easy entry. I was right: my rose had done the trick—almost too well. Doug was so "tickled" that only seconds after his entry into my hot box he was shooting his load of cum.

Doug got such a bang out of it that I could hardly complain about my not achieving an orgasm with him. His skin was all hot and wet and beet red; Doug was that excited. I know how torturously ecstatic tickling can be. It's like an itch you want to scratch and scratch, yet you don't want it to go away. With tickling, particularly if you're tickling a man with a flimsy feather rose, the sexual excitement is so close, yet so far. It feels good as those soft feathers caress his cock, but he definitely wants more, more than any soft feather rose can offer. After a while he can't help wanting the soft, yet firmer featherlike texture of your love tunnel. Ultimately I knew Doug would have to take me, whether I wanted it or not, though of course, I wanted it. But I also wanted a good healthy orgasm of my own. Now that he'd spent his seed, how was I going to get myself off?

Doug rolled over, pulling himself out of my crotch. Oh, I wanted him so much now. The ostrich feather bedspread was still tickling my back and buttocks, and I wanted to relieve the pleasurable pain of all that itching, tingling, tickling feeling. "Please, Doug, get me off," I begged. And I grabbed his head, lowering his face to my crotch.

"Hold it a second," he said. "I've got a better idea." Oh no, I thought, another anticunnilinguist. Another male chauvinist orgasmist, only interested in his own climax. Screw the woman and leave her begging. "Just give me a second," he whispered. "I've got a surprise that's a whole lot better than my eating your quim."

"What if I don't like your surprise?" I whimpered. "What then?"

"Then I'll lick your quim till you're sore."

Doug stepped into his walk-in closet and closed the door behind him. I wondered what kind of masturbating gadget he had in store for me. Behind the closet door I heard some loud, snapping noises, and I thought he was probably fastening some superdildo to his hips. I began contemplating the wonders of modern science. Without them, what would a horny woman do? After all, nature had certainly played a dirty trick on the sexes, giving women boundless sexual stamina and limiting mortal men to merely one orgasm per screw.

Just when I was beginning to wonder if Doug would ever reappear, the closet doors opened. Doug was standing there nude, but I couldn't see any plastic emerging from his crotch, just a leather strap around his waist and thighs. Then I noticed something dangling from behind him. It looked like more ostrich feathers, but how could it be? Then he turned, giving me a good look at his body profile. The leather straps around his waist and thighs were holding a big, long ostrich feather tail attached to his buttocks.

I was too surprised to speak. I guess my mouth was wide open because Doug said, "Shut your mouth, and hop on my back." Doug was a lot heavier than he had looked in his slimly styled clothes. I grabbed the feather tail which seemed to emerge from his buttocks. It was good and sturdy and thick, with the feathers fastened onto a leather base. I jumped on his back, wrapped my legs around his hips, and grabbed onto his shoulders, gently resting my crotch on the tail. The ostrich feathers tickled my pussy, and I had to giggle. "Here we go!" Doug yelled, and with that he started hopping around the room. The tail jerked up and down against my crotch, the feathers tickling my pussy and thighs. It fitted snugly against my vaginal lips, and as Doug hopped around the room, it vibrated against my clitoris. With the feathers tickling me and the leather stimulating my love button, I was climaxing within minutes.

I didn't want to stop, though, and with my legs wrapped around Doug's hips, I soon felt his erection against my ankles. Oh, he was hard again, and as Doug hopped next to the bed, I jumped off his back and onto the ostrich feather bedspread.

As soon as I landed, I spread out my legs and held out my arms. Doug entered me again, but it was even kinkier this time because he was wearing the feather tail. While he sank deep into me, I grabbed onto the tail and fondled it until we both climaxed together.

Of course, I had to ask Doug where he'd got the idea of wearing a feather tail. "Oh, just an idea of mine," he said. But I knew he was concealing something. I could tell by the sheepish grin on his face.

"Oh, come on," I said. "Someone must have given you at least an inspiration."

"Oh, it comes from an old affair. A lover of mine had this thing about feathers and being tickled, so I designed this feather tail. When I saw you in the store, fondling the feathers on that dress, I thought you might appreciate my little fetish. Also, I've read your books and I know what a tolerant person you are."

I appreciated the tact of that word, "tolerant." I tried prying even further, to see whether or not Sara Star was actually the inspiration for this feather-tail fetish. But Doug wouldn't tell. I soon put Doug and Sara out of my mind, even though I could never quite erase that feather experience from my memory. How strange, when merely a month later, I was sitting in a movie theater with Brigitte, watching this phantasmagorical costume epic, and Sara Star appeared on screen in a cameo role wearing a feather tail. It was a dream sequence, and she was supposed to be the embodiment of evil and decadence: one-third woman, one-third she-devil, and one-third bird.

Then I knew for certain that Doug had used Sara Star's fetish to feather my nest that night.

All in a Lather over Leather

My girlfriend Brigitte and I had taken an automobile trip to Paris, but we were there only two days when I had to make a quick return to Amsterdam to settle some business. Brigitte remained in Paris, and I drove back alone. Now one might think that a woman traveling solo from Paris to Amsterdam would encounter a number of horny hitchhikers willing and eager to screw. Not true. Most hitchhikers are tired and have only one thought on their minds: How am I going to get from here to there?

Keith wasn't any different. I picked him up about an hour out of Paris. From a mile away I could tell he was an American kid; his sneakers and jeans jacket were dead giveaways.

"To Amsterdam?" I asked him, and he jumped right in, throwing his small duffel bag in the backseat.

"I can't believe this," he said. "No rides, no sleep in two days."

A typical hitchhiker, I thought. Too tired even to try. Oh, well, I'd just have to wait until I got to Amsterdam. I expected Keith just to fall asleep in his seat. I'd leave the kid alone and let him get some rest.

I was driving along, minding my own business and not paying much attention to Keith, when I felt his hands on my jacket sleeve. I'd just bought the leather jacket in Paris a few days before. It was a very stylish jacket, and at first I thought Keith was admiring its cut. Then I noticed the manner in which he was feeling the leather. His fingers kept running over and over the same area of the sleeve, and the boy's eyes were practically in a trance. Keith's mouth was slightly open. Yes, this was a guy with a heavy leather fetish.

"You like leather?" I asked, smiling.

"Oh, excuse me," Keith said, pulling his hand away. "I guess I got a little carried away. My leather jacket was stolen a few days ago. I don't have enough money left to buy another, so I have to go back to the States in this denim shit." Then he gazed at me like a genuine leather junkie. "You know, I really like chicks in leather, particularly skintight black leather. I'm a motorcycle freak myself, mainly because I like the babes on the bikes. Naturally a lot of these chicks wear black leather for protection against burns or accidents. Leather has its practical side if you're a cyclist. But the kind of leather I like chicks to wear is really skintight stuff—nothing bulky or loose."

He paused for a few seconds, looking at me as though he needed some kind of fix. "You don't mind my touching your jacket, do you?"

"Of course not. Tell me, what's the sexual attraction of leather on a woman?"

"I can't really say," Keith whispered, fingering my jacket sleeve. "It's associative, I suppose. Cycle chicks also like their men to wear leather. Maybe you don't know that when a chick sits behind her man on a cycle and puts her face into his leather jacket, she associates the leather smell and feel with her guy. The same is true for the guy with the chick. I've had a leather-clad chick on my back while riding my Harley. We'll be going eighty or ninety down the freeway when I feel her leather glove reaching into my chaps, hunting for my hard-on. Soon your erection starts vibrating right along with your machine. Motorcycles are pretty sexual machines; you feel all that energy pulsating underneath your crotch. When you've got a chick on your back, though, and she's feeling you up with her leather glove, it makes it all the more exciting."

"But what about the *feel* of leather?" I asked. I'd slept with a few who requested I wear some leather to bed. Certainly it was an erotically charged material, but I could never figure out why. "What's the sexual appeal of leather?"

"There's something malleable, yet very tough about leather," Keith explained. "When a girl wearing leather rubs up against your cock, it feels so tough, yet so tender.

"My favorite outfit for a girl is tight leather pants, leather jacket, gloves, and boots. It's the only costume for a cycle bitch. Sometimes I get on the cycle behind her. She drives, and my crotch slides down her leather back and snuggles up around her leather-encased ass. I feel up her hard leather tits, stomach, and pussy. Sometimes I even open my trousers so that my bare erection can run up against the leather covering her ass. There's something strong and sexual about leather. That's the fetish."

Keith was silent for a while. "Would you like to hear a story about a couple of leather freaks?" he suddenly asked. "Actually I was one of them."

"Why not?" I said. "It sounds interesting already."

Well, Keith began, there was this special chick who loved riding bikes, but her boyfriend couldn't stand her wearing leather gear. "I remember meeting her at this cyclists' club. I had all my leather on. Most other people did too, but she was wearing a faded denim outfit. Still, I found her attractive as hell. Her boobs were positively spilling out of her denim jacket. Hell, she wasn't even wearing a blouse underneath, and her left nipple was peeking through the spaces between the buttons. You could tell by the deep tan on her boobs that she was a practicing nudist, and I get off on that sort of thing.

"I kept looking at those flimsy buttons. It looked as though they might pop off any moment. Nothing could have pleased me more. Maybe I should help those buttons out, I thought. But I was too timid.

"Her midriff was bare, and she had an 'innie' belly button—just the kind I like. I kept thinking how beautiful her wide, full hips would look in some tight black leather. Her hips were swaying from side to side as she walked across the club. Too bad the denim slacks just didn't do those buns of hers justice.

"I had to meet her. I'd never forgive myself if I didn't. Finally, I got up enough guts to walk over to the bar and ask if she'd like another beer.

" 'Yeah, a Heineken, please.'

" 'I haven't seen you around these parts,' I began. 'You don't live near here, huh?'

" 'No, my old man and I are just riding through on our way to the cyclists' convention in Thompsonville,' she said, taking a slug of beer from her bottle.

"My heart sank to my ankles. Chrissake, wouldn't you know it? The foxiest chick in the whole place, and she has to have her old man with her. I shrugged, trying not to act disappointed, but I guess my face isn't a good liar.

" 'Hey, don't be so glum, man.' She laughed. 'Just because I've got my man with me doesn't mean I can't play around.'

"She took another gulp of beer, and I took a deep gulp of barroom air. I'd always fantasized about meeting some chick and saying point-blank, 'Hey, would you like to go outside and fuck?' but I've never had the courage. Fortunately, this chick believed in cutting through all the preliminary bullshit. I admire that in a woman, and I knew I had to have her.

" 'So where's your old man?' I asked.

" 'He's standing over there.' And she pointed to this big bruiser across the room. 'Hey, Mac, get your ass over here. I want you to meet somebody.' Mac slowly got up from a stool where he was chatting with a couple of women. He walked over to us. 'Hey, Mac, this is my friend . . . hey, kid . . . what's your name.'

" 'Keith.'

" 'Keith, this is Mac and I'm Janie. Mac, Keith and I are going to split for a while. I'll be back here around ten, okay?'

"Mac smiled a sheepish grin and said, 'Nice meetin' ya, Keith,' and he walked back over to the two girls he'd been talking to. Now *that's* what I call tolerant.

"Janie and I split. We had our choppers parked out on the street. I hopped on mine, and I expected Janie to get on behind me. Instead, she got on her own bike and insisted that I sit behind her. 'It'll be better this way,' she said. 'I never like riding on a cycle when I'm not in control.' And off we went.

"The ride through the city was the wildest I'd ever experienced. Every cop in town must have been off duty that night. It felt like we were cutting through those alleys and streets at about sixty miles an hour. Janie was a nervy broad all right, and I didn't want her to think I was chicken, so I hung on for all I was worth. I kept thinking, though, how much more exciting the ride would have been if she'd just worn black leather. I nuzzled my nose down into her shoulder and thought how much I missed that good leather smell mixed with a woman's perfume and body scent.

"I hung onto her hips. Like I said, Janie's hips were wide and full, and riding on the cycle with her, I sank my fingers deep into her. It was a great big soft ass, and I knew my hard-on would fit nicely in its crack. I pushed my pelvis forward so that my crotch was right next to her ass. My dick grew hard immediately, and I was so close to Janie that she couldn't help feeling it rise and tickle her behind.

" 'Hey, watch it!' she laughed. 'You don't want me to come while I'm driving, do you? Safety first.'

"Safety first? Hell, we were barely missing fire hydrants and streetlights as it was. I pushed my crotch away from her, but my erection wouldn't deflate. Luckily, she wasn't wearing leather, or I'd have shot my wad for sure.

"Janie drove out of the city onto this lonely little dirt road. I'd lived in the city for a year, and still, I'd never been down this road.

" 'Mac and I came through here this morning, and we balled on that spot—over there.' And she pointed to a grass-covered hill near a riverbank. 'We whizzed by here, and I saw that hill, sitting up there like a bed, and I said to Mac, "Let's ball, baby." It was such good sex I've been itching to try it out again. Come on, let's go.'

"That's one thing I like about cycle chicks—they don't mind being the aggressors if they feel like it. And Janie certainly was that. If only she'd been like most other broads on bikes and worn black leather.

"Janie took me to her grassy hilltop for lust under the stars. I grabbed her denim jacket and pulled at the two loose buttons entrapping her boobs. God, I'd waited all night for that. I gave them a good tug, and her suntanned breasts came spilling out. Janie took off her jacket and held her breasts up for me to see and kiss. Not that she needed to. Her boobs were firm and stuck straight out on their own. Her nipples were already hard. They were big chocolate-brown ones, too, like giant-size candy kisses, ready to eat. I sucked on them, pinching them gently between my teeth as I started working on her jeans. She must have put her jeans on with an aerosol can, they were so tight. Oh, if only they were leather! It is such an incredible high, rubbing up against a woman's soft, tender skin and at the same time running your hand over smooth, tough leather. It's as though the leather is protecting her from harm. The woman in leather is wearing armor, in a way, and in order for me to screw her, I must break through that armor. Somehow denim just isn't the same thing. It doesn't have the same challenge.

"I tried tearing off Janie's jeans, but they were too tight. I had to settle for peeling them off her body. The snap on her jeans broke, and her round, yet firm little belly plopped out. Damn, she was wearing underwear, black underwear. Didn't like that. Never known a cycle chick to wear underwear of any kind. Then I grabbed her big ass and felt something much tougher than black nylon covering those buns. I couldn't believe it! Janie was wearing skintight black leather panties! I grabbed her quim and felt a good healthy bush of pubic hair. God, custom-made leather panties! These babies were crotchless, too! I could make love with Janie and satisfy my leather fetish at the same time.

"Janie tried taking off her wild panties, but I motioned for her to keep them on. She seemed insistent that she remove them, so I had to throw her back on the ground and enter immediately. Now there was no way she was going to get those leather babies off. Not with my dick in her.

"My hard-on was throbbing in her sweet tender vagina as my hands rubbed against her leather-covered ass. Of course, I kept on all my leather gear—the black leather jacket, my pants, even my heavy boots. Except for her panties, Janie was naked, and all this leather made me feel all that much more powerful against her soft, suntanned skin. I felt like I was wearing iron and screwing this voluptuous maiden through a chink in the armor. What a contrast! My hard leather gear and her wet, soft vagina. Even the sounds were wild—the crackle of leather and the quiet gurgling noises of her crotch.

"When we were finished making love, Janie told me how her old man, Mac, just didn't appreciate leather on his chick. 'He says it's not feminine. But I like leather, and so I wear these black leather panties. I had them made to-order at a place that specializes in this sort of thing. Mac doesn't mind too much. It's a compromise. What he can't see doesn't hurt him. And when he *can* see them, I take them off.'"

Keith relaxed against the seat after finishing his story, and I thought, "Now he's going to catch up on his sleep at last." But suddenly he came to life.

"Hey," he said, "why don't we screw in the backseat of the car? But you have to promise to keep your leather jacket on."

I was game—and pretty soon the two of us were going at it hot and heavy. Maybe Keith had something at that because we were certainly all in a lather over leather long before we finished.

Erica Jong, You Were So Wrong!

Usually I can't sleep on airplanes. I suppose that's why I've laid so many guys up in the air; there just isn't much else to do. I've forgotten how many times I've had some guy follow me into the john at twenty or thirty thousand feet. It's really not the best place to have sex—the quarters are just too cramped, and there's no real thrill at the danger of being caught in the act.

A more adventurous airborne screw took place on my last flight from Toronto to Amsterdam. During a screening of *What's Up, Doc?*, I simply put a blanket over my lap and the crotch of the young male passenger next to me, and we proceeded to masturbate each other for three thousand miles.

My best sex in an airplane didn't really take place at all. What I mean is, I fantasized it, partly while I was awake and partly while I was asleep. I was flying from Amsterdam to Rio de Janeiro for the Carnaval '77. It was such a long flight—fourteen hours—that even I slept for at least a few hours. And that's when it happened—I became a living fruit basket! In the dream, of course. I've known people who've had fruit fetishes and couldn't have sex unless they and their partner also got it on with some fruit—like grapes in the vagina or bananas up the anus. But I surpassed them all in my fantasy.

We'd been in the air over the Atlantic Ocean for six hours. I was eager to see Rio and to enjoy the warm summer climate. It was sunset, and the clouds were like little white sheep grazing over the horizon. The drone of the engine had me practically hypnotized, and I was going to doze off at any second. Then the door to the control room opened, and out walked the captain. He was dressed in blue with gold braid, and his epaulets made his shoulders look enormously wide. His body formed a perfect V that met at his slim hips. I loved the uniform, but I wondered what his body looked like underneath. Was it padded, or was this guy for real? If only he would turn around so I could check out his ass. Then he did turn around, and there before me, not six feet away, were these nicely rounded little muscular buns covered in blue with not an inch of material to spare. He was talking to one of the more unattractive stewardesses, and as he talked, he started shifting his weight from one hip to the other. It was as though two little piggies were fighting in his seat as his buttocks rubbed against each other underneath that tight blue material. I could feel my crotch begin to dampen. My mouth dropped open, and I could feel my tongue grow heavy. What was I going to do? I needed something right then and there. Squeezing my legs together wouldn't work. I thought of running back to the john to work off my frustrations, but I didn't want to miss the show of his tight little ass muscles flexing themselves right before my own steamed-over eyes.

I grabbed a blanket from the overhead compartment and spread it over my crotch. With his ass wiggling, I started working my finger around as though it were his cock up in me. Closing my eyes, I imagined him inviting me to his cabin for a nice little orgasm somewhere thirty thousand feet over the Atlantic Ocean. The engine was droning on; the other passengers were fast asleep, not that I cared if they saw us or not. If he wanted, I'd have obliged him with a quickie in the aisle, but this captain was a private man, and so in my dream he invited me to that cabin in the sky for sex at thirty thousand feet altitude.

The control panel was lit up like a Christmas tree, but still, it was a fairly dark room. The moon was full and overhead, and below I could see the tiny whitecaps on the ocean. He started to unbutton his uniform. His chest was muscular and hairy. I started to get wet again. Controlling myself, I said, "Wait. Why don't you leave it on? It's a little chilly in here anyway." Not that the cold night air bothered me any as I stripped off my dress in record time. God damn it, this was *my* fantasy, and I'd always wanted an airplane captain—and that meant he was going to keep his uniform on while we screwed his eyeballs out. Otherwise, he'd be just another naked man. I wanted to finger that gold braid, feel his pounding chest beneath that blue uniform while he sank himself deep into me.

I unzipped his pants and lowered his uniform trousers. He wasn't erect yet, so I took him into my mouth, running my tongue down his soft shaft until it started to rise. In no time I could taste that good salty taste of semen as it oozed ever so slightly from the head. Afraid that he might come too soon, I took his balls in my mouth, flicking my tongue against them. He laughed and begged me to stop. "You're tickling me to death," he said, laughing. I paid no attention to him. This was going to be a spot of oral sex he'd never forget, and I didn't care if he did die laughing. Many have come to a worse end in life. So I kept diving at his balls with my tongue, giving him the old butterfly kick against the testicles. His laughter and crying got louder and louder. All of a sudden . . . God, the door burst open . . . and in walked this homely stewardess he'd been talking to before.

"Is something the matter, Capt—" She looked white. "Oh, my God, my God, what's going on here?"

The captain straightened up immediately. He zipped his fly, pointed at me, and said, "This woman barged in here and started blowing me like crazy." It was the same voice he used over the intercom. My crotch throbbed spasmodically, and I came immediately. "I was just too stunned to do anything about it," he continued. "We'll have to take care of her."

She nodded, pivoted around on her flat heels, and hurried out the door. I stayed at his feet, wondering what these people would do to me. I didn't move. I worshiped this airplane captain, and I certainly wasn't going to put my clothes back on. Whatever the punishment, my blow job had been worth it. The homely stewardess returned with a male steward carrying a bowl of fruit.

"Turn her over the seat," ordered the captain. The steward obeyed. As he lifted me, I didn't resist. He sat me down on the seat so that my ass stuck up in the air. Chains were placed around my ankles and wrists. I was helpless, completely at their mercy.

"Start with an orange in her mouth," ordered the captain. "I want her silenced. When she starts screaming, I don't want the other passengers to be alarmed." An orange was promptly shoved into my mouth.

"Maybe this will teach you to stop blowing off airplane captains," snarled the ugly stewardess, and she whacked me hard across the ass.

"Try squeezing lots of oranges against her breasts and crotch," said the captain, "so that her skin gets all sticky and gooey from the juice. After you've finished that job, you can try shoving a few sliced pears up her." He looked at me and, for the first time, he smiled. "You know," he said to the stewardess, "there's nothing like sticking your hot organ into a woman who's been saturated with lots of juicy pear slices."

The steward smiled, his white teeth gleaming. I started to squirm. I certainly hadn't embarked on this trip to become the captain's fruit salad, but I was powerless. I could do nothing at all to defend myself from the treatment accorded me by this demented threesome. I could feel it harden against my nipples. The juice flowed freely down the crack of my ass, and it wet my pubic hair. Soon my blond pubes were a golden orange. Then came the sliced pears up my crotch. I had to admit to myself that they felt so tender and nice up there in my hot box. In no time it felt as if they were melting. I clamped my legs together to make them dissolve even faster. At first it felt so mushy, then I could feel the pear juices intermingle with my own until they flowed freely from my crotch.

The steward had me spread my legs so he could suck those pear-flavored love juices from my vagina. He couldn't lick and gobble and suck it up fast enough, but the captain pushed him aside.

"And now for the best of all," he said softly into my ear. Unbuttoning his trousers, the captain let his erection pop out at me. Slowly he glided it into my vagina, his penis moving smoothly alongside all those melting pear slices. I felt so full, so satisfied, yet so hungry for more.

I pushed my crotch against his so that his entire cock would sink into me. I could feel the pear slices inside me and his erection sliding in and out against them. My crotch was gurgling so much, and the scent was like a beautiful perfume. The captain kept giving it to me. My vagina sounded as though I were ready to explode from being stuffed with fruit and rammed with this man's erection. And yet I wanted more . . . more . . . more. . . .

"More? Did you say *more*, Miss Hollander?" It was this stewardess—the ugly one—she was standing over me with a basket of fruit. "Would you like some fruit?" I was back in my seat with the other passengers. My fantasy dream was over! The airplane captain was nowhere in sight, and this homely woman was offering me fruit. "We'll be landing in an hour. Would you like some fresh fruit for breakfast? A banana, maybe?"

No, thanks. I was pissed as hell that I'd fallen asleep and lost track of my airplane captain. Then again, my fetishist fruit dream had been so good! How could reality ever compete? When you've creamed the impossible dream, why ruin it by trying to have your banana and eating it, too?

VI. Xaviera's Magic Mail

One of the biggest turn-ons for me is reading my morning mail. Now I must confess that the postman does bring me more in that pouch than just your average batch of bills and advertisements. True, I get those, too, but interspersed with the more tedious aspects of usual mail is some of the best erotica ever set on paper. I guess I just inspire the kind of confidence that leads to true confessions.

Readers from all over the world write me about their sexual experiences and often ask me advice in dealing with related problems. The letters I've chosen to print here, since this is a book on fantasies, are mostly those from fantasists who've either acted out their fantasies or are planning to do so. This can be a real problem, so I've offered these writers my best advice on how to win the fantasy game. The letters I've chosen are about some of the most common sex fantasies. In this case, however, common is never dull.

The letters may turn you on. They might even shock you. Then again, as you read the letters, you may very well find some fantasies surprisingly similar to your own.

Bushwhacker, Beware, or A Clearing in the Underbrush

Dear Xaviera:

I'm a housewife, twenty-five years old, and I have one child. My husband and I had a pretty good sex life before the child, but now he seems to be completely obsessed by a strange sex fantasy. You see, right before I had the child, my gynecologist shaved my pubic area. Well, since my delivery, my husband, David, has been trying to keep my bush shaved. He just loves the sight of a naked pussy. I resisted and resisted, telling him that I did not fantasize about a prickly pubic area, and since I was the one who'd have to live with it, the answer was definitely no.

That was six months ago. My refusal to shave my pubic hair, however, just about ruined our sex life. Having seen me "bald" before, my husband just couldn't get it up any other way. I guess his sex fantasy got the better of him. Finally, I had to give in and shave my patch. After all, his impotency had been going on for two months.

At first we agreed that he was only to shave the lower part of my bush so it wouldn't look as though I'm completely bald down there. Every few days my husband would coax me into having him shave and trim my bush. We actually developed a little sex fantasy ritual. It would go something like this:

The night begins by having a nice hot bath and

several drinks. After bathing, I put on a long black nightgown that David purchased for me. As soon as he sees me in it, his prick gets rock hard. He takes me into the bedroom, slips me out of my gown, and begins fondling and sucking my breasts until my nipples are quite hard. Then he starts on my toes, kissing and licking me all the way up to my wet hot box. He spreads my legs about as far as they will go and then applies warm shaving cream to my lower bush. He begins shaving me very slowly and carefully. I have to admit that the feeling is unbelievably exciting. Just the thought of him looking directly into my box gets me off.

After he has completely shaved my asshole and pussy, he neatly trims the remaining hair with a hair clipper. He then cleans my pubic area with a very warm washcloth and carries me into the bedroom. When he goes to the bathroom, I watch his throbbing dick bounce up and down. I lie there completely nude, shaved and trimmed, knowing he is coming back into the bedroom to eat me. When he returns he begins licking and drilling his long hot tongue into my soaking wet pussy and asshole until I come again and again. We finish with me on top, exploding together, filling me with more and more of his loving fluids.

Don't get me wrong. I really love these little bush-whacking parties very much, but there are some problems. If my husband had his way with this fantasy, he would have these parties every night. Unfortunately, a day or so after one of these shaving sessions, my pubic area becomes quite irritated. What can I do about this?

My other problem has to do with the appearance of my pussy. I like just the bottom of it shaved. I prefer the hair on top simply to be trimmed, not because it makes me feel sexier, but because of the fact that when I'm standing up nude with my girlfriends, for example, no one knows I'm shaved. The only time you can tell my pussy is shaved is when I'm lying down in the nude with my legs spread wide. The only people who see me in this position are my husband (no problem there) and my gynecologist. The doctor is the problem. I'm afraid my doctor will think me some naughty or cheap whore if he examines me and sees this shaven pussy. Right now I only let my husband shave me after I've made a visit to the gynecologist. Should I feel this way about my examinations? I certainly don't want to sabotage my husband's fantasy. I'm beginning to like it myself.

An admirer,
June

Dear June:

Your husband is the one who counts most, my dear. If he wants a completely "bald" pussy, and you don't really mind, then by all means oblige your man. I wouldn't worry about your gynecologist. Sometimes we women have too much respect for our doctors. Remember, you're paying him, not the other way around. What's more important to you: your doctor's respect or your husband's well-being? A good doctor is easy to find; a hard husband is another story. Stick to the man you love. His fantasy is a rather mild one with few bad side effects.

However, regarding the itching effect on your pubic area, I'd take your husband's advice: try shaving your pussy more often. Soon it won't itch. I vacationed last winter in Brazil for Carnaval '77, and since I was wearing a little bikini all day long, I thought it more becoming to shave my pubic hair just a bit. Of course, in a day or two my crotch felt unbearably itchy. Finally, I just shaved my whole pussy naked. It itched at first, but with the help of some baby powder and baby oil, I was able to relieve the irritation. For the next few weeks I shaved my pubic area every other day and found that the itching subsided and soon stopped altogether.

When I returned to Amsterdam, however, and started wearing more than bikini bottoms, I let my bush grow back. Wouldn't you know! I met a young art student named Jack, and with my bush now fully redeveloped, he thought it appropriate to use my pubic hair and his tweezers as a brand-new art medium. His sex fantasies, like his art, ran something to the abstract, and so after an hour's work with his tweezers, I had a triangular box, or should I say, a triangular pussy? The next morning Jack reshaped my pubic hair into a box—for my box—and by nighttime there were just a few tantalizing hairs surrounding my clitoris.

Try expanding upon your husband's sex fantasy. The next time your husband wants to enact one of his shaving fantasies, why don't you surprise him with a *dyed* pussy? What a treat it would be for him, when he goes to cut your blond or brunette pubic hair, to find a flaming red pussy.

Be imaginative. I remember one Irish girl who, on St. Patrick's Day, not only dyed her pubic hair green but cut them into the shape of a cloverleaf. Of course, if you're not quite so bold, you can take a tip from the girls at the Crazy Horse Saloon in Paris. They wear pussy wigs, called *merkers*, that are dyed to match the color of their dyed head wigs.

You might even try a red heart pussy for St. Valentine's Day; red, white, and blue pubic stripes for the Fourth of July; and a platinum-blond snowflake for Christmas.

Pussy hairs can also be used as a means of suggestion. Let's say you want more shopping money. Your crotch as a green dollar sign might do the trick. Indeed, there's a world of fantastic possibilities. Your problem is not as hairy as you think.

Ball in the Family

Dear Xaviera:

I'm thirty-two years old, and I have a thirteen-year-old son. I've always considered myself a good mother, and I can't believe that I'm now fantasizing about incest with my child.

My husband was among the MIA in Vietnam, and I have long since given up all hope that he might still be alive. My mother-in-law lives not far from here, and for that reason, along with my husband's uncertain fate, there have been no other men in my life. I'm good-looking, have a beautiful body, and, frankly, Xaviera, I'm horny as hell. For the past six years my sex life has been a world of fantasies, masturbation, and vibrators. And now this thought of sex with my thirteen-year-old boy!

These incestuous thoughts began a month ago when my son had an accident trying to jump a fence at school. He got a bad cut in the groin, right next to the scrotum. In the emergency room the attending physician advised me that the dressing should be changed daily. I had not had any occasion to see my son's penis since he was about ten years old, and at that time it was a tiny little wiener. The first time I was to change the dressing, I don't know why, but I wasn't prepared for his fully developed penis. When he stretched out on his bed, I touched him, and his penis stiffened immediately. I sucked in my breath. I had never thought of him as a sexual being, just as a baby boy.

"Oops!" I gasped. "I hope I didn't hurt you." He calmly said no and explained that it was a natural reaction because I was so beautiful and my soft hands felt so good. He didn't appear to be at all embarrassed. I was the one who was flustered, shaking and trying to deny my own sexual arousal. I told myself that this could not be happening, that I was a mother and this was my son. But there it was—the first fully grown and erect real live penis I'd seen in six years—and it was staring me right in the face. I tried, but I just couldn't resist wrapping my hand around it, bending it slightly to one side. It felt heavenly. I watched the scrotum and testicles draw up toward the body, and I almost had an orgasm. I finished dressing his wound as quickly as possible, and then I left the room immediately.

I tried to busy myself with little jobs around the house, but the picture of his husky, muscular, and tanned body with that perfectly shaped ivory cock sticking up in the air had burned itself into my brain. That night I even dreamed about my boy's penis.

The next day I suggested to him that if he could change the dressing himself, it might be less embarrassing. He tried, but soon he called for me, saying that it was in such an awkward place that he couldn't manage it.

This time I tried being nonchalant, but his penis immediately popped up hard. I quickly cupped up his balls in one hand and ran the tip of a finger down the length of his penis. "You've grown into quite a man, haven't you?" I whispered.

"Yes, ma'am," was all he could say. My boy just kept smiling at me.

After a minute of my playing with him he asked if he could question me about something. I said, of course, but I wasn't prepared for his question.

"Mother," he began, "does a man's penis really feel as good going into a woman as people say it does?"

I almost started to reprimand him for asking me such a thing when I stopped myself. After all, the boy no longer had a father. Who in the hell was supposed to tell him about sex? So I finally told him that it probably felt better than what people had been telling him. "Especially," I said, "if the boy and girl are in love." Then he wanted to know, "Doesn't it feel good even if you weren't in love or married?" I had to say yes because I just couldn't lie to him.

Xaviera, I've fantasized so much about having sex with my boy. I'm asking you to put yourself in my position and then to give me an honest answer. I'm thirty-two, and I haven't been to bed with a man for six years! Think now, if you were sitting where I'm sitting right now and that young, vibrant penis was only a few feet away in the next room. Wouldn't you find a way to rationalize having sex?

For every rule, there's an exception, and I believe my situation is an exception. I see no reason why an incestuous relationship with my son could not be beautiful and beneficial for us both. Without another male in the house, I believe it would be much better for a young boy to be introduced to sex in the security of his own home without guilt, fear of discovery, unwanted conception, or disease.

While struggling with myself over this decision, I have had a maddening desire to compromise by simply fellating or masturbating my son. Terrible guilt feelings have so far restrained me from what I really want—to make love to my son, to have his erection in my vagina. What advice can you give me regarding my fantasy?

Yours,
A Puzzled Mother

Dear Puzzled:

Your problem is not one of incest fantasies. You simply need a good loving man to care for you and make love to you.

As you write in your letter, "I have long since given up all hope that he might still be alive." So what are you waiting for? A few hypocrites may question your behavior, but most people—those who're true human beings—will welcome your company. You may feel somewhat guilty at first, but you must make a choice: avoidance of your initial guilt or a loving man. In time your emotional needs will win out, and you'll correctly choose the latter. Why wait any longer?

As for your mother-in-law, she would surely understand your wanting a man. If she doesn't, then I'd ignore her false loyalty to her son.

Regarding your incest fantasy, however, I must offer a few words of caution. Sometimes our sex fantasies are not quite what they appear to be. From your letter, I don't think you really want an incestuous relationship with your son. You just want cock, and understandably so. Your son just happens to have the most available penis in the house. Before you try seducing your son, find yourself a man; that's what you really want—and need.

SM—It Isn't a New Brand of Cigarette!

Dear Xaviera:

I have always found sadomasochistic sex fantasies abhorent. I've heard and read about stories where women want to be chained up and whipped by their male lovers. Maybe I'm an overly civlized man, but somehow such activities just sent shivers up and down my spine. Certainly I never found such sex games erotic. I can't remember ever having gotten an erection from such sights or thoughts.

But that's before I met Jenny, and I suppose that's why I'm writing to you now, Xaviera. Tonight I've been sitting here in the office for hours, wondering if I should write this letter. It's really about Jenny and her wild, screwed-up sex life. In fact, I'm at her desk now, thinking of her. I met her eight months ago when I came to this firm. I was twenty-three, fresh out of graduate school, and she was a secretary of twenty—tallish, slender, with brown hair and lovely brown eyes, a nice figure, and a wonderful personality. I think I flipped for her when we first met. Who'd have thought that her sex life evolved around bondage and slave-master sex games?

I'd never even thought about SM sex fantasies before meeting Jenny. Now it's all I fantasize about. As of yet, however, I haven't indulged in any of her games.

XAVIERA'S FANTASTIC SEX 167

At first Jenny and I got along fine, but I could never understand why she dated Drake. He was about her height—about five-eight—and slender, but he looked seedy even though he had a decent job. He generally picked her up after work, and that's when I first met him.

When warm weather came, Jenny began wearing tank-top-type blouses. One day I was near her desk, at the file case, and I turned to find her bent down toward the typewriter. Her blouse fell forward, so I looked. Her left breast was a cute sight all right, but the little metal ring, pinched hard on the nipple, threw me. I couldn't figure out why she would be wearing such an uncomfortable, if not painful, clamp against her soft flesh. Jenny glanced up and realized what I saw. She blushed but said nothing.

It wasn't my business why she was wearing this little metal ring, so I said nothing. But a few days later I began getting suspicious when I overheard her on the phone speaking to Drake: "Please, not that way again, Drake. I'm sorry I offended you. I promise I'll be good." When Drake picked her up that evening, she looked very pale.

A week later I attended the damnedest party of my life. A friend invited me, and he said the party would blow my mind. So at nine that Saturday night I walked into his house and found about ten guys sitting around with ten girls. Each girl was nude and had her hands bound behind her. One guy had one hand in his girl's cunt and the other on her nipple. In a corner a cute redhead was blowing a guy. Another girl in the kitchen was getting screwed in the ass. Most of the guys in this place had whips with them.

Then I saw Jenny. She was a naked beauty. Unfortunately, Drake was with her, and it looked as though he'd just finished screwing her. Her eyes were damp, and red lines were visible on her buttocks and hips. She blushed when Drake led her over to me. "I've heard about you," Drake said. "Take her for a couple of hours." And he gave Jenny and his whip to me. Drake laughed and then turned away. Probably to pick up some other chick.

I spent the next two hours making love to Jenny in an upstairs bedroom. No whip. No games. She was tender and warm, and her response lifted me to heaven. In between lovemaking we lay close, and she told me she belonged to Drake forever. I said I didn't buy that. She kissed me on the chest, saying that I was too kind to understand. "You are very, very wrong." Jenny sighed, and then she began to cry.

And, damn it, I was. I love her, she knows it, but still, Jenny goes off with Drake. I've been back to that party once more, and again I made love to Jenny. I guess that was Drake's idea of torment—letting me have her for an hour but no longer. Jenny is still all his.

Honestly, this is all I know about their relationship. And my question is, why? Is there any chance Jenny will leave that creep and lead a decent life with me? If not, should I enter her fantasy life to play her SM games?

Sincerely,
Jim

Dear Jim:

I doubt if you're really cut out for Jenny's style of SM. From your letter, you seem to be partial to a more conventional and less hassled form of lovemaking. Nothing wrong with that. Different games for different gents. But let's be realistic. If you were to win Jenny's affections, she'd probably find your style of sex rather boring and you'd continue to abhor SM. You two are just a bad match, sexually.

I think you're oversimplifying Jenny and Drake's relationship. Do you truly think Jenny is Drake's unwilling slave, that she is performing these SM games against her will? Maybe Jenny would be a happier person if she were not playing the slave role, but then why does she wear a little metal ring around her nipple? If Drake were forcing her to do so, it wouldn't be necessary for Jenny to wear the ring to work.

I know how possessive some men can be, but the days of white slavery are past, Jim. If Jenny really wanted to leave Drake, and she felt as though her very life were threatened, I'm sure she'd look to you for help. But she hasn't.

You write that you've always been "terribly abhorrent of SM sex fantasies," but I don't think SM fantasies are your problem, Jim. Instead, you seem to be more prone to the most common sex fantasy of all: desiring someone you can't have. I could be wrong. This is something you'll have to examine on your own, but would you find Jenny so attractive if it weren't for her "forbidden" sexual relationship with Drake? It has been said that pity and love are almost identical emotions and that some people can't tell them apart. Is this the case with you?

Jenny is a masochist in need of her master. Reexamine your own emotional involvement with Jenny, and I'm sure you'll find the two of you to be quite incompatible.

Pushing Your Instant-Replay Button

Dear Xaviera:

My story is a little unusual, Xaviera, and so I'm writing to you. Perhaps you know differently, but I haven't met anyone whose experiences duplicate mine.

Last year, when I was promoted to associate professor, I got a good pay increase, so my wife and I decided to step up our standard of living. The first thing we did was to move into a brand-new apartment. The day we moved in, another couple was moving in right across the hall, and there was some joking about our furniture getting mixed up. My wife, Marylene, and I liked this other couple instantly, and so we asked them out to dinner. We were immediately on a first-name basis.

The moving had taken place on a Saturday, and the next Thursday Marylene invited our neighbors, Max and Lila, for dinner in our apartment. We started out with a couple of martinis before sitting down to one of Marylene's super dinners. During the meal the four of us managed to knock off a couple of bottles of wine, and by the dinner's end we were all feeling pretty high. Somewhere along the line the conversation got into sex; at times it even got a little raunchy. Max had some unconventional ideas on sex, and much to my surprise Marylene agreed with him. Really, I'd never thought about such things as wife swapping, but there Max and

Marylene were, discussing the benefits of switching partners.

By this time I was really on the fuzzy side from all the wine, and when the other three agreed to having a sex quartet, I just went along with the idea. We went into our bedroom, where Max at once undressed my wife. At first I felt awfully possessive of Marylene, but then I thought, what the hell. This is partner swapping, after all. I turned to Lila. Since my marriage to Marylene, I had done no outside screwing. All of a sudden the idea of extramarital sex seemed very desirable, indeed.

By the time Lila and I undressed Max and Marylene were already on the bed in a 69 position. While I watched, I couldn't believe how professionally Marylene swallowed his cock. Lila and I were soon doing the same, right beside Max and Marylene on our king-size bed.

When Max swung around and started screwing my wife, I did the same to his wife. This Lila was an extremely hot number, and she'd already had an orgasm from my oral work on her pussy. I suppose if I'd been cold sober, this orgy wouldn't have happened, but maybe not. At any rate, it was intensely exciting to lie there pumping away at Max's wife while I watched him wildly screw mine. In some ways it was the greatest sex I'd ever had, including my loss of virginity.

I think Max and I went off simultaneously, and we fell back out of our partners onto the bed. Lila immediately rolled over to Marylene and began kissing and caressing her, with full reciprocation from my wife. I can scarcely describe what I thought or felt when these two women went into a 69 position. Marylene a lesbian? It didn't seem possible, yet there she was sucking out Lila's pussy.

Max was stretched out next to me, and our naked

bodies were touching. I tried moving over, away from his body, but the bed wasn't quite *that* large. Max said, "Hell, what's sauce for the goose is sauce for the gander," and he just plopped right down and pulled my cock into his mouth. I was in such a receptive condition that I didn't even reject what he was doing to me. In seconds I had a flaming hard-on. He was amazingly good at it, and soon I was floating on waves of desire. If he'd stopped, I would have asked him to continue. He was squirming around on the bed and all of a sudden, it seemed, there his cock was—hard as steel and poking in my face. I was trembling with fear and excitement when Max said, "Go on, eat it," and he pushed his tool to my lips. And I took it!

Never in my life had I had a homosexual experience or even a homosexual fantasy. I had never even desired another's man cock, yet there I was, sucking cock. And sooner than I would have thought, Max and I were having our second orgasms in each other's mouths.

All four of us rested, and then the women got up to check into the bathroom. After they left, Max rolled over and said, "I get the feeling this is all new to you."

"It sure is," I said, laughing. But I didn't feel any revulsion. Apparently I had accepted a facet of my sexual nature I hadn't known existed.

"One helluva lot of guys are missing one helluva lot of fun." Max grinned, and without saying more, he kissed me smack on the mouth and went down to work on my cock some more. I couldn't believe it, but my cock was erect again, and soon Max was offering me his. I didn't hesitate this time. I simply took it in and blew him for all I was worth.

When Max and Lila had left, Marylene said, "I was surprised to see you sucking Max's cock."

"No more surprised than I was to see you eating cunt," I replied, adding that it was the first time I'd ever had a homosexual experience. She couldn't say the same, though, and confessed that she and Lila had been eating each other since the previous Monday.

"Lila is irresistible," she said.

"So is Max," I replied. Then and there we agreed to accept what each of us had done. I'd never before had three orgasms in a single session; to tell the truth, I didn't think I was capable. Needless to say, I gave a lot of thought to what had happened, but the strangest part was the feeling of pleasure I had in remembering it. Had I been unconsciously gay all along without knowing it? Yet I knew I wasn't really gay either. My zest for cunt remained *and* remains.

The next Sunday afternoon Lila came over and said Max was trying to fix a wobbly chair. "He's not much of a carpenter," Lila said with a laugh. "Could you please help him?" So I went over to help him out while Lila visited with Marylene.

Well, there was no wobbly chair, only a very hot male wanting male sex. He got it, and I got a strong lesson in what one man can do with his mouth and tongue to another man's genitals and anus. When I left Max that afteroon, I was carrying two of Max's loads in my stomach, and I'd given him two drinks of my semen. Later on Marylene and I had the greatest session in bed we'd ever had.

The following Tuesday my education continued when I went downtown to have lunch with Max. He is a very successful corporation lawyer, and his office was very luxurious. We sat talking until his secretary announced that she was going out for lunch. Max immediately locked the door and started to strip. I was jittery. I was afraid his secretary would come back and catch us bare-assed. Max laughed. "No big deal if she does," he said. "We'd just add her to the fun. But she won't. She's too wise for that."

This time our sex was different. I sat on what he called his "client's sofa" with my legs spread wide while he knelt between them and gave me a buildup suck. Then we changed places, and I sucked him off, my cock getting even harder than he'd left it. Next, he pulled me down to the floor onto his back as he guided my willing cock into his asshole. I just pushed it in and screwed him like mad. That was the first time, too, but far from the last.

Under Max's guidance, I've screwed and been screwed a number of times, but only with him. Now that I've become pretty adept at swinging and partner swapping, I'd like to try myself out on some other couples, but I feel a little strange about it. The question I keep asking myself is: Have other men had this type of experience?

Wondering,
Bob

Dear Bob:
Of course they have. But like so many men who have just experienced their first foursome, and their first homosexual sex, you might feel a little guilty, and therefore, you think your experience is unique. Well, it's not. This is one of the reasons I've written this book, to show people how normal most fantasies are.

How lucky you are, Bob, to have met such tremendous "teachers" as Max and Lila. They've taken the aggressor roles and gradually introduced you and your wife to new forms of lovemaking that have enhanced your own sex life within marriage. If you want to experiment further, try asking Max and Lila to set you and your wife up with some other couples. I suggest, however, that you invite Max and Lila to accompany you on your initial outing alone. Just to break the ice, so to speak. Obviously, they're experienced swingers and must know lots of other people. But be careful. No one can guarantee you that those other partners will be anything like Max and Lila. You take your chances.

I find this letter particularly interesting because Bob details one of the most common forms of fantasizing. Bob writes: "When I left Max that afternoon, I was carrying two of Max's loads in my stomach, and I'd given him two drinks of my semen. Later on Marylene and I had the greatest session in bed we'd ever had." Bob also writes: "Needless to say I gave a lot of thought to what had happened, but the strangest part was the feeling of pleasure I had in remembering what had happened."

Obviously Bob has spent a lot of time fantasizing about his sex with Max; these are what I call recapitulation fantasies. Everyone wants to re-create some great sexual experience from his or her past, but to do so may be impossible. People move away and are no longer available to you. Also, your own experiences sometimes make it difficult for you to recapture certain states of mind. Even if you could set up the same circumstances, chances are you can never recapture that old magic. Better to start anew and try something different.

Fantasizing about old experiences, however, allows you the opportunity to relive some of those prize moments and to excite yourself sexually at the same time. As with Bob, you may fantasize about your first sexual experience with someone, playing the episode over and over again in your mind. Perhaps you'll even improvise on it somewhat. Take Bob's experience, for instance.

I'm sure he was quite uptight when he first had sex with Max, and I doubt if there was much verbal play. In his imagination, Bob can now improve on their initial sex by adding verbal sex talk. They can tell each other how big their cocks are, how good their sperm tastes, et cetera. All this will help excite Bob when he's alone or perhaps when he's with someone else. Of course, this is all in Bob's imagination, but that's where the libido begins.

Sharing Sally's Sex

Dear Xaviera:

Xaviera, I used to be the most possessive man in the world. My wife, Sally, couldn't look at another man without my getting upset. I'm really ashamed of how I used to act, but that's all changed now. Today I masturbated twice just fantasizing about Sally getting laid by other men.

Sally is a college student, and one day she and a cousin of mine named Rick, who lives with us temporarily, met me at a restaurant after Sally's classes. During dinner I suggested that we all go out together. Sally said her midsemester exams had been tedious and she would certainly enjoy a break, but where should we go? I mentioned that there was a club, the Powerhouse, which had an excellent boogie band and it might be fun to dance a little.

We took Rick's car. When we arrived, they dropped me off to reserve a table while they parked the car. Inside, we had a great time, drinking several rounds of beer and dancing almost every dance. When it was time to leave, we were, as Sally put it, "considerably enlightened." Sally and Rick left to get the car, but I remained behind for just a few moments to congratulate the musicians on their new record release. Finally, it was closing time, and I left to look for the car.

I searched around for a while, but the only blue Volvo I could see had a couple making out in it. Then I took a second look at the car, and sure enough, it was Sally and Rick. I waited for a minute. God, could this be my own wife and cousin kissing right there in the parking lot? When they finally withdrew, I approached and knocked on the window. They let me in, and we drove home as if nothing had happened. I wanted to knock Rick's block off, but I was just too angry even to speak. I'd have to talk to Sally when we got home.

All of a sudden I began feeling sick to my stomach. As soon as Rick parked the car in front of our apartment building, I ran inside. I was afraid I was going to vomit, so I waited in the bathroom. I don't know how long I was in there—it must have been at least a half hour—but gradually my queasiness disappeared. I walked to our bedroom, expecting to find Sally there, when I heard noises coming from Rick's room. A small light was coming from under the door. I knelt down very quietly and looked through the keyhole.

The two of them were standing there completely naked, silhouetted by a single candle, as they firmly grasped each other's thighs. Their kisses were long and heavy, and I could actually see their tongues entangle. At first I wanted to break the door down and slug it out with Rick. It's what I should have done, I remember thinking, back in the parking lot when he made a pass at Sally. But now I had a hard-on as I watched them kiss and fondle their naked bodies. It was a raging hard-on, too. It actually hurt, I was so hot. I couldn't believe how aroused this little lovemaking scene had made me.

My hard-on just wouldn't stop. It had to be relieved, even before I did anything to either of them. And so I whipped out my erection and started jerking off as though my life depended on it. I kept watching through that keyhole, though. They were still in a standing position when Rick's penis got hard and he put it right into my wife. God, my wife! The mere sight made me so humiliated and so hot that I just shot off immediately.

I guess my orgasm was so loud—I tried to muffle it—that Rick and Sally heard me. Rick threw Sally on the bed immediately and opened the door. There I was—my hard-on in hand with cum flying all over the place. I was so embarrassed, but Rick wasn't. He just looked down at me and said, "Well, if you're going to see it, you might as well see it all."

As I entered, I noticed a small rubber mat on the floor. At one end there was a squeeze bottle of baby oil and at the other end a small saucer. Rick knelt down, but Sally remained standing. She looked frightened, but Rick finally coaxed her into "performing." I should have stopped this, but the strange thing was I didn't want to stop it. Even though I'd just come, my penis was rock hard and hurting again like hell.

There was silence as they both stretched out on the mat. Lying head to foot, side by side, they proceeded to massage each other's legs, working slowly up toward their crotches. Finally, Sally rolled over on her back and spread her legs. Rick followed on top of her, and their mouths lodged on their excited genitals. As they sucked feverishly, each coated their fingers in the oily substance and held their hands outright. Rick lifted his head slightly and said, "Now." At that they proceeded to insert their index fingers up each other's anuses. The hotter they got, the more fingers they added. Finally, they had three fingers frigging their assholes as they ate out each other. With a pang of pleasure, Sally arched her back and began her first orgasm. Rick looked as though he were about to come, but he pulled his penis out of Sally's mouth and entered her vagina. Within seconds Rick came, his body racked as though in convulsions.

I watched this all in silent amazement. Of course, I masturbated again even though there was no more sperm in my body. I was so excited, however, that my penis would not go soft. I kept thinking how hot Sally's vagina would be after having been just screwed by Rick. What the hell! After all, she was my wife, and so I entered her on the spot as Rick watched. It was incredible sex.

As a husband I suppose I should have knocked Rick's block off. Instead, I begged him to keep servicing my wife so that I could watch. Sally and Rick can't understand my reaction, but now we all seem to be enjoying ourselves. In fact, it's gotten to the point where the three of us have staged orgies with Sally and several other men.

I still remember the first Saturday-night party we had. Six guys showed up. None of them believed Sally would perform the way Rick and I said she would. But when they left, none of them was walking straight. I took lots of snapshots and got some fantastic pictures of Sally and the guys. I've never seen so much cum on one chick in all my life. The best pictures show Sally kneeling on the floor with four erections all aimed at her face with two hard-ons in her mouth at the same time.

Well, after the Saturday-night party, we agreed that there should be more of these orgies. The problem we ran into, though, was that more and more guys kept showing up. So far the guys have all been neat and clean, but there are getting to be too many men. Some men even come by when I'm home, begging for a blow job or a screw. I want Sally to have a good time, but I don't want the guys interfering with my own sex life. Sally doesn't either, and she's told them all to wait until our Saturday-night parties or to come by during the day when I'm at work. A couple of times guys have begged Sally to the point where she's had to go out to their cars and blow them then and there.

Even though our lives are infinitely more hassled than before, I enjoy having such a sexually active wife. Is there something wrong with me for wanting her to screw so many other men?

Worried,
Carl

Dear Carl:

I receive many letters from men wanting to watch their wives in sexual intercourse with other men. Such an episode happened quite by accident for you, and because of your former attitudes toward machismo ("I used to be the most possessive man in the world"), you seem to have found your act of voyeurism quite humiliating. Perhaps you were afraid of being a cuckold—or more likely, afraid of wanting to be a cuckold—so you went overboard to the point of being "the most possessive man in the world."

Emotionally you enjoy being humiliated ("the mere sight got me so humiliated and so hot"), so why not try some physical humiliation as well? True, there are those masochists who merely enjoy the emotional pangs of humiliation, not the physical "abuse," but you might give it a try.

Sally and Rick seem open and kinky enough to oblige you. Try a sex fantasy scenario like this:

You watch Rick and Sally screw. Then, when it's your turn to make love, you begin but Rick pulls you out of Sally and says, "Wait a minute. She's my woman, and I don't want her screwing around."

"But she's my wife," you say.

"So what? No other men's pricks in her, just their tongues," Rick commands. Since you are his obedient servant, Rick punishes you by spanking your butt, while you lick his cum from Sally's vagina.

That's just a sample of what you might try. You'll think up your own variations the more experienced you become at SM.

I wouldn't try the SM games, however, at one of your orgies, at least not until you're more experienced. First, try them out on an experimental basis in a controlled setting with Rick and Sally, two people whom you know and can trust. Later you might introduce your SM sex fantasies to the group.

By the way, why should Sally always be the center of attraction? Other men probably share your fantasy. You might try inviting some more women to these group sex parties. You shouldn't spread Sally too thin!

VII. The Washington Capers, or, Federal Fantasies from My Forbidden File

When I was a New York madam, a naïve call girl of mine once asked, "What's considered kinky sex in Washington?" I replied, "Just plain getting laid."

On the whole my acquaintance with Washington officials and politicians was a rather straight affair. As a sexual lot, these men and women tended to want their sex without any kinks and with little imagination.

I've never discussed or written about any of the Washington, D.C., clientele I had as a madam and call girl. This was no oversight. In the past I've been afraid that any accusations involving members of either the Johnson or the Nixon administrations might ensure my deportation from the United States. Even after I moved to Canada, I still thought there might be some hope that I would be allowed one day to make a return visit to the States. Last year, however, I was deported from Canada, an action which all but destroyed any hopes I had of returning to America. With this in mind, and a new administration in Washington, I now feel it's time to publish that all-important, yet missing chapter from my memoirs.

In John Dean's book *Blind Ambition*, it is strongly intimated that Nixon's press secretary, Ron Ziegler, often frequented my brothel. To quote Mr. Dean:

Ratnoff [a consultant for the Knapp Commission] had also managed to copy Ms. Hollander's address book. But there was *another* address book, for sensitive political people, and it was not known whether Ratnoff had it. . . .

. . . I [John Dean] began asking the more adventurous men at the White House if they might have anything to fear from Xaviera Hollander's address book. When I whispered my story to Press Secretary Ron Ziegler, his face went white as a sheet. "I'll deny it," he said quickly. "I'll deny it." He turned and walked away. But over the next few weeks Ziegler kept up a steady stream of calls to me, asking for further developments. His tone was so urgent I could scarcely keep from laughing. There were no further developments, except that Ms. Hollander did quite well as a public figure.

John Dean should be so lucky. Some prostitutes are professionals; others never learn. If Mr. Dean wants to name names, he should check out his facts. So far I've not received any calls from the man.

My brothel in New York City was a business, and my clients trusted me—as they would a lawyer or a doctor—to keep our transactions private. For that reason I'll never name names, but if I may not be so brazen as Mr. Dean, I can certainly tell you more about some politicians' sex lives—and those they fantasized about—than John Dean ever dreamed.

The following six stories are among the more memorable Washington tales I have to tell. Just call them my Federal Fantasies.

The Strange Case of the Meatless Master Spy

My first Washington caper took place shortly after I began working as a call girl for Madeleine, one of my first New York City madams. One evening I was feeling very tired and decided not to check the action at Madeleine's brothel. Instead, I just stayed home and watched Humphrey Bogart treat Ingrid Bergman like a whore in *Casablanca* on the tube. Somehow real prostitution was never quite that glamorous. Right after Ingrid asked Sam to play it again, the telephone rang. It was Madeleine, and she needed help. I was going to tell her to find another girl, but she sounded frantic. A Washington official was in town, some dude from one of the capital's intelligence agencies, and he was with his *male* lover. I'd read his name in the newspapers, and of course, I had no idea he was homosexual. I felt a slight shiver run through my tired body. Somehow, there was no thrill like discovering a celebrity's true sexual persuasion.

"So, if he's gay"—I giggled—"what the hell do you need me for? Call up Frank or Jimmy for a stud."

"Please, Xaviera," Madeleine pleaded, "would you just get yourself over to the Hilton? I've got problems over here at the house, and no way can I do this job myself. You're the only I can trust to bring it off. All you have to do is watch these men make it while you masturbate yourself. Don't even touch them; just make sure, though, that you all have simultaneous orgasms. Got it? Oh . . . Room Twelve-thirty-seven-A."

And then she hung up. I had to go, of course. Madeleine's place sounded like bedlam. Maybe it was a police raid. Also, checking out this scene with Mr. Eye Spy and his lover boy sounded very intriguing.

The New York Hilton had always been one of the tougher hotels for prostitutes to enter, so I dressed as a sweet young stenographer with eyeglasses for this trip. When I got to the twelfth floor, Mr. Eye Spy's guards were there, and I gave them Madeleine's name. Leeringly, they directed me to the appropriate suite. My disguise obviously didn't fool them, but still, I wondered if they knew about their boss' gay scene and my part in it. For that matter, maybe they even knew more than I. After all, who ever heard of a female prostitute being called to two gay men's hotel suite?

Mr. Eye Spy's male lover answered the door. "Where's Madeleine?" he asked. "I asked for Madeleine. What happened? Who're you?"

After introducing myself, I tried to explain the circumstances. "I think Madeleine was having problems with the police," I said. "You know how the government can be about these matters."

Somehow this guy and I didn't share the same sense of humor.

"Look," he said, letting out a big breath, "did Madeleine explain *everything* to you?" He nodded as though to emphasize the word "everything."

Nodding my head, I stammered, "Why . . . why, yes. She did."

"And whatever you do," he continued, "don't say anything to *him*!"

Him? He said the word as if it were part of a hellfire and damnation sermon. Fine with me. I'd just as soon not talk to either of them. But where the hell was Mr. Eye Spy anyway? And why was this hotel suite so poorly lit? If I didn't know better, I'd say I was frightened. Washington politics was foreign to a girl from Holland.

I was then asked to strip and follow Mr. Eye Spy's lover to the adjoining bedroom. Just one tiny blue light was on in the corner, and it took my eyes a while to adjust to the semidarkness. I did notice, however, that the lover was also now naked and leaning over the bed. Something seemed to be moving on the bed, and after much blinking and squinting, I finally made it out to be some form of human life. Obviously, it had to be Mr. Eye Spy himself, and what a sight he was! His lover wasn't bad for a middle-aged man. In fact, I rather fancied him myself, with his firm stomach muscles and neat little ass. But Mr. Eye Spy! As Marlene Dietrich in *Touch of Evil* told an obese Orson Welles: "Honey, you're a real mess. You've been eating too many of those candy bars." I was going to make a crack when I remembered my manners and my promise to say absolutely nothing.

Instead, I positioned myself beside their bed so I could watch them. I was really expecting some freak scene out of the Marquis de Sade's *Philosophy of the Bedroom*, but instead, I got *The Hardy Boys Get Lost in a Hayloft*. I just couldn't believe it!

The lover grabbed Mr. Eye Spy's penis (very small; no wonder he had a Napoleon complex), he in turn grabbed the lover's, and together they proceeded to jerk each other off. I felt this was my cue to perform, so I began masturbating my clitoris. It was then that reality surrendered to *their* fantasy.

As soon as I began fingering myself, the two men turned their faces to my crotch, and they immediately began talking dirty to each other. But this wasn't any old kind of bedroom dirty talk, for these two homosexuals were such closet cases that even to themselves they wanted to fantasize heterosexual sexplay.

Now I've known gay men who feel they have to lay a woman once a year just so they can make their claim to be hetero or bisexual. But these two Washington types *never* got it on with chicks. They'd just hire a prostitute once every few months to have her masturbate beside their bed while they jerked off. As they did each other, these two would talk as though they were both having intercourse with the prostitute at the same time—one in the vagina and the other up the girl's anus. The one night I made it with them—if you can call it that—their fantasy dialogue went something like this:

"Do her good, up that hot cunt of hers." The lover groaned.

And then Eye Spy said, "Yeah, and does her ass feel good to you?"

"Oh, she's the best I've had in a long, long time." The lover sighed, manipulating the other's penis between his fingers.

"She's good and tight up front, too," said Mr. Eye Spy, taking a better grip.

His lover grabbed his balls and again groaned. "I'd just love to ride her good and hard, all night long."

"Oh, her body is so hot that I can't . . . I can't hold it back. Come, come with me. Come with me. Are you ready?"

"Yeah, I can't wait!"

"I'm . . . I'm coming, too. Don't hold it. Don't hold it back."

"God, I'm going to shoot in her. Man, this is like I've never shot before!"

I naturally took all this orgasmic talk as my signal to come along with them. Actually, I felt nothing in my crotch, even though they were screaming about how good and hot I was. When I began to mimic their cries of orgasm, I was not prepared for what I was to see, for both men immediately grabbed some facial tissues and covered each other's erect and throbbing penises. Not only were they hopeless closet cases, but they were also cleanliness freaks! It seemed that oral and anal sex was far too unwholesome for these two guardians of the American moral fiber! For their sake, I just hoped they didn't get arthritis. It would ruin their sex life.

They lay in each other's arms for a moment, and then the lover got up and escorted me out of the bedroom. As I put on my clothes, he thanked me for coming and apologized for his earlier rude and abrupt greeting. "You see," he said, "we just don't like to do it with a different girl each time. You understand." I just smiled, shook his hand, and quickly walked out the door. Halfway down the hallway, I could have hit myself for not picking up the tab. I turned back to their hotel suite and then remembered that such "dignitaries" were always too genteel to pay for it in person. (Remember, this was my first Washington caper.) Rather, they would pay—or had already paid—Madeleine for my services.

When I got back to my place, I called Madeleine. She sounded in somewhat better shape than when I talked to her earlier. She'd paid off the cops and got the other girls calmed down somewhat.

"So how'd it go?" she asked. "Pretty freaky fantasy, huh?"

"Yeah, real freaky. For fifty bucks it wasn't worth the trauma."

"Well, just remember, Xaviera," she said, "that fifty comes out of my pocket. You know, these guys don't pay for it."

I couldn't understand it. What did she mean, "They

didn't pay for it"? It was then that Madeleine gave me Lesson No. 1 in American politics. As she explained it, many of these high officials in Washington's intelligence agencies could do exactly as they pleased because they had all the inside dope on everybody. If some U.S. senator was about to challenge them or expose their corrupt tactics, all these officials had to do was make a friendly telephone call to inform the senator that either his son was gay or his daughter was hooked on heroin. No one would know, if Mr. Senator would just play their game.

"So I play their game, and they get a free screw. After all"—Madeleine laughed—"I only have to put up with them a couple of times each year. Just think if you were working in Washington, D.C., the year round?"

That was all right for Madeleine, but when I ran my own peanut stand and it became my turn to mastermind these Washington capers, I charged—and charged plenty. As you'll learn in the following pages.

Caper No. 2:
South of Her Border

Luckily, Mr. Eye Spy and his male lover were exceptions to the general Washington rule. The top intelligence people played their own game, but most of the government people I knew were generally a very discreet lot and paid their bills in advance—no complaints and no hassling of the merchandise. I'm certain this was more a tribute to their fear of blackmail than to their sterling character. No Washington official ever came to my brothel; they always asked for my outservice. Even so, it has always been difficult for such prominent people to have illicit sex without at least a few people knowing about it. After all, how do you get around all those guards and Secret Service men around your hotel suite?

One White House bigwig was so worried about gossip that he'd subtly "bribe" his guards with a little sex, on the house—the White House, that is. Naturally, such timid officials as Mr. Bigwig were a godsend for my girls. With a dozen guards and Secret Service men around, one of my girls—at a hundred dollars a hit—could make a killing in just one night. She might have been a little tired the next day, but with that kind of a gang-bang, the girl wouldn't have to lay again for a week.

I remember my first call from Mr. Bigwig. Usually Washington officials would have their private secretary call, but not this pussycat. He was much too afraid of gossip, and so in the dozen or so times he dealt with me, Mr. Bigwig always made personal calls. At first his request was simple: "I want the girl to be Spanish, and not an American citizen." His latter qualification was typical of many government dignitaries. They often wanted foreign girls who wouldn't recognize their names or faces. Unlike Madeleine and many other madams, I never told my girls a famous john's name. I'd simply give the girl the client's address and any special instructions regarding his sexual preferences or kinks.

In this first call from Mr. Bigwig, he told me he'd be staying in New York City for the weekend, and he requested a different Spanish girl for each night. "These girls will also be servicing my personnel," he added. "About eight men altogether." I asked if he wouldn't prefer that I send over at least two girls an evening—to ease the load, so to speak. But he was adamant and insisted on one girl an evening. "Remember, she must be Spanish." And then he hung up.

That weekend I sent Mr. Bigwig three of my finest call girls—all of whom were from Latin America. Upon reporting back to me, all three girls had somewhat similar and slightly disappointing stories to tell. Each said that sex with the security men was great and that the guards seemed to be enjoying it. However, sex with Mr. Bigwig was rather perfunctory, and he was noticeably disturbed about something. Only when they had sex with the security men did he seem to really enjoy himself. "You mean, he watched while you performed sex with his guards?" I asked, not quite believing it myself. Indeed, he did! And all three told me the same story.

I soon forgot about the incident, but four weeks later I received another phone call from Mr. Bigwig. He thanked me for his previous "dates" and said he'd be in New York City for just one evening later in the month. "I need a girl, but she *must* be Spanish," he insisted. "You know . . . *Spanish*. Also, I'd particularly like it if she had an accent. And couldn't she wear makeup?"

I thought a moment. The first three girls were Spanish, they all had accents, and they wore makeup. Why hadn't any of them lived up to his Latin lover fantasy? Then I remembered. When a man says he wants a woman with makeup, he doesn't mean the low-key look. He wants red ruby lips, black mascara eyes, two or three beauty marks, and lots of cheap rouge. If he wanted a whorish-looking prostitute, well . . . I'd give him a real Forty-second Streetwalker.

Fortunately, no such girls ever worked for me, but as any prostitute knows, many men pay for sex because they enjoy paying for sex. It's not that they can't get it any other way; they just like knowing that their money buys a woman—if only for a few minutes. Such was Mr. Bigwig's sex fantasy; however, he didn't want just a prostitute—he wanted a nympho bitch!

Since we had no such girls, I needed an actress. Lori was one of my best call girls, she was studying with Lee Strasberg, and she was Spanish. While a student can always use more money, I often sensed that Lori was more into prostitution for the sex than the cash. For this assignment, I coached her on how to be a real Eighth Avenue streetwalker. I picked up a red satin dress for her, some mesh stockings, and a pair of black high-heeled shoes. Lori barely had an accent, so I asked her to bone up on her Spinglish lingo. (Actually, she was from one of Miami's better families and hadn't been any farther south than Key West.) Last but not least, her name had to go. For Mr. Bigwig Lori would be rechristened Carmen. After all, this was *his* fantasy, and it was costing him plenty.

Finally, "Carmen's" big night came, and I sent my self-manufactured Spanish spitfire *puta* off to meet her big-shot date. When Lori called me early the next morning, she sounded exhausted—understandably—but excited. In fact, she couldn't stop giggling. "Xaviera, I deserve an Oscar for this!" she said, laughing. "At first I was a little insulted, being treated like some streetwalker. Then I decided to really get off on his whole fantasy, and so I started in with 'You want me to suckee or fuckee?' "

I was all ears. "So what happened?" I asked eagerly.

"He went wild, Xaviera. I wasn't prepared for this kind of crazy, wild animal. He just lifted up that red dress and ripped off my black lace panties. I tried to get my dress off, but I guess he wanted it on 'cause he took me right there. I mean, we did it with all our clothes on standing up! It knocked the breath out of me completely. Not because he was so large—he wasn't—but he just took me with such force and so damn fast that I couldn't collect my thoughts. When I got hold of myself, he'd already shot his wad. Then he invited these four guards to take me. One right after the other—wham-bang-bang—they did me while he laughed and laughed about what a whore I was. Then, when they'd all finished, he screwed me again. Xaviera, I'll never forget what he said. 'I just want to screw you so I know what it feels like—what a *puta* feels like.' Isn't that funny?" And she burst into convulsive laughter.

From past experiences with Lori, I knew from her giggles she'd had a good, horny time. Controlling her laughter, she added, "You know, Xav, when he finished with me, that Washington bigshot put a dollar bill on the table and said, 'Now pick that up like the *puta* you are!' I hardly knew what he meant; then I remembered that scene in *Lady Sings the Blues* where a prostitute picks up the money with her vagina. Xaviera, I have never had this much fun in acting class! Too bad Strasberg wasn't there."

Lori, in fact, was such a success that Mr. Bigwig asked for her every time he came to New York. Occasionally, I even flew Lori to Washington for one of his special parties. After she'd gang-banged his husky guards and given Mr. Bigwig a second round, he'd always throw Lori that dollar bill, ordering her to pick it up with her "lips." His fantasy may have been that she cost only a dollar. In reality, his fantasy cost a cool six hundred dollars each trip—all in the White House. But that was another administration. I have a hunch the new one couldn't fantasize a scene like that even if it tried. And maybe it's just as well!

Caper No. 3:
The Senator with the
Two-way Letch

At the time I was servicing Mr. Bigwig, I also knew a newspaper reporter, Michael, who was a friend and customer at my brothel. One evening we were watching the evening news together and playing around on the living-room coffee table. Michael was a real swinger, bisexual *and* beautiful, but like Mr. Bigwig, he liked to pay for his sex. I used to kid him that he'd screwed every girl in my place and every guy in Tommy's male whorehouse. "Don't you ever want it for free?" I asked, tickling his feet.

I wasn't really watching the television set, but all of a sudden something caught my eye. It was this gorgeous senator from somewhere west of the Appalachian Mountains. Washington types had always struck me as either asexual or just plain boring, but this guy was beautiful. Tall, dark, and then some. Since Michael was a newspaper reporter and knew a lot about Washington politicians, I asked him if he had any dope on this guy's sex life.

"Oh, that senator." He chuckled, nibbling on my toe. "I made it with him and his wife at the national convention last year. Not a bad swinging duo, either." Excited as hell, I pulled my toe out from his teeth and asked him to tell me the whole story. The *whole* story!

"Well, it was late one evening on the convention

floor," Michael said, grabbing my left foot. "I was very tired when this senator's wife approached me. I recognized her from various news releases and pictures, and so I introduced myself. After a little chitchat she invited me to a party she and her husband were throwing in their hotel suite. She was a tall, beautiful woman with a slim model's figure, and I was attracted to her immediately. Still, I was tired and it was late. But she persisted. She even started cooing in my ear about how much she and her husband wanted to meet me. 'We've admired your work so much,' she whispered. By now her knee was rubbing up against my thigh. I could hardly believe it! We were right there on the convention floor, for chrissake! I got an erection just thinking about the circumstances. As soon as she felt my hard-on, this woman threw her head back and laughed. 'I knew I'd get to you! We'll see you around twelve.' And she handed me a sheet of paper with the address on it."

As it turned out, Michael did go to their suite to attend what he thought would be a boring party. He naturally expected their room to be filled with dull conventioneers, but surprisingly their suite was empty, except, of course, for the senator and his wife.

Instinctively Michael blurted out, "So where's the party?"

Senator and Mrs. Swinger laughed and said in unison, "You're it!"

Michael turned pale. He was flabbergasted and felt he wanted to evaporate on the spot. Yet these two very attractive people seemed so relaxed and so at ease that Michael himself began to cool off.

"You see, Mike," the senator began, "oh, by the way, you don't mind if I call you Mike, do you?" He didn't wait for Michael to respond. "My wife and I have noticed what an excellent job you're doing on the convention floor. You're obviously a man with a big career ahead of you. You're also a man of discretion, and I'm sure that we can trust you." The senator looked at his wife, smiled, and then started talking again. "We watched you and thought maybe you were a swinger, too, Mike. That you probably made it with both chicks and guys, right?" Again, Michael wanted to respond, but the senator kept right on talking. "Since you're like us in that you do have a career to protect, we thought it might be safe, not to say fun, to have a little three-way tonight."

Michael looked at the Senator's crotch and noticed that it was bulging. Also, his wife's legs were apart and Michael could see right up her short skirt. "Well, what do you say?" she asked, smiling. She was smoking a cigarette, and to Michael's eye it looked as if she were masturbating it with her lips and hands.

Michael wanted to say something, but he didn't know what. "May I use your bathroom for a second?" he finally asked. "I just need to get myself ready." Senator and Mrs. Swinger laughed, moved in their seats, and looked at each other with their tongues hanging out.

When Michael came back from the bathroom, he was surprised to find that the senator's wife had left the room. As it turned out, the senator was almost exclusively gay except for occasionally servicing his wife in a three-way combination with another man. Usually the wife had sex with other men, men she had picked up, much as she'd found Michael. She had a reputation around Washington as being very promiscuous, when in fact she was just acting as a panderer for her husband. The senator could not go around cruising for his own men, so the solution was for her to pick up the men— always respectable career men who were as susceptible to blackmail as they. If the men turned out to be straight, they were hers for the night. If they were bi, then they'd have a threesome. Gay men were her husband's property. While Michael was bisexual, it seemed that the senator had pleaded with his wife that he be left alone with this prize catch.

"After all," explained the senator, "my wife's biggest sex fantasy is just acting as my go-between. She has more orgasms picking up my men than actually screwing them. Ever since she saw Elizabeth Taylor act as Montgomery Clift's sex decoy in *Suddenly Last Summer*, she's wanted to be a female pimp. I was just the man to complete her sex fantasy."

The two men had a few more nightcaps before actually hitting the sack. Somehow Michael had expected such a powerful statesman to have a much larger penis. Silly, what misconceptions people have of power and genital size. Still, in Michael's mind it seemed only appropriate that he should be the active sex partner that night. When the senator saw Michael's much larger erect member, there was no quarrel, and so with practically no foreplay, he immediately threw his long, lanky legs up into the air for Michael to sodomize him. Michael saw no jar of K-Y or Vaseline in sight, so he rimmed the man's ass and spread his own saliva over his hard organ. He slid it in with absolutely no problem. Obviously, this powerful senator was experienced in more than one kind of floorwork. Sliding his penis deeper and deeper into him, the senator's anus contracting against his hard thrusts, Michael cradled him in his arms until they were like one hot and throbbing animal.

In thirty minutes their sex was over, and soon they were nestled in each other's arms. The senator somehow seemed much less demanding of Michael after sex than when they'd first met. In fact, now he was even begging Michael for a favor. What a fantasy-come-true this was! Here Michael was, a layman (literally and figuratively), having just sodomized a powerful politician, and now that politician was practically his servant.

"Please, Michael," he whispered, "you will do this? Tomorrow? My wife has always wanted anal intercourse. It would be her dream come true . . . really! She's always been a little afraid of the pain. I've tried to take her anally, but somehow anal intercourse is just something I do with other guys. Please?"

So the next night, after the convention, Michael found himself with his greased penis between Mrs. Senator Swinger's sweetly plump buttocks. He tried being gentle with the woman. After all, he was deflowering her anus, so to speak. Michael had always said he never cared to perform a sex act on a married partner if the other spouse had not done it with them sometime previously.

"It's the first rule of swinging," Michael said. "The passive spouse often gets jealous." He felt particularly hesitant with these two, but then, the wife was practically begging for it.

At first Michael was gentle. But after a few slow thrusts she asked him to do it harder and faster. "Come on, Mike, do me good and hard, like you did my husband last night. I can take it, too."

With her legs spread in a wide V formation, Michael watched his hard penis slide in and out of her crotch. With each thrust she gasped for air, only to ask for more and more. "Please, harder . . . harder!" That rough he'd never done any man, but it was what she wanted.

Michael performed like an obedient servant, taking her anally with absolutely no mercy. The senator watched and masturbated as his wife was sodomized by this near stranger. It was their fantasy-come-true. As for Mike, he'd been around a bit. But he had to admit it was the most unconventional convention he'd ever attended.

Caper No. 4:
The Lesbian Who Was Made to Lie—and Lie and Lie

Lesbian sexplay is probably the most common fantasy of heterosexual men. In fact, in almost any swinging situation, it's rare to find a man who does not want his own wife or girlfriend to make it with another woman.

I remember one U.S. diplomat—I forget which banana republic he bought his way into—who used my call girl services on a regular basis when he was in town. His male secretary would call me, asking that I send two girls to the ambassador's East Side town house. The secretary's voice was so low and husky and sexy that I almost hoped he was calling for himself. I've generally found telephone voices to be misleading, but then let's just say it's one of *my* sex fantasies.

I'd heard about some pretty wild parties at the ambassador's town house, and so I asked the secretary if the girls were for Mr. Ambassador or for a party of men. When the secretary said they would be "just for Mr. *and* Mrs. Ambassador," I knew this was one trip I shouldn't miss.

I'd seen Mr. Ambassador's picture in the papers—a little mouse of a man with a white shock of hair. He had to be at least seventy. Nothing there. But Mrs. Ambassador was an altogether different story. *Women's Wear Daily* was always featuring her as the hostess of a ball or featuring her latest wardrobe. I didn't much care what her clothes looked like; I wanted the woman underneath those high-fashioned rags. She had to be less than half her husband's age, and from her photos, Mrs. Ambassador looked like a mature *Vogue* model: high cheekbones, dark, hooded eyes, and straight hair that fell down her slender white neck. She had always looked so cold and unapproachable from those photos that I wondered what the real woman was like. And I've always wondered what young, beautiful women see in men ready for the retirement home. It had to be money, or so I thought. Where else but in politics were such antiques not forced to retire?

Suzi was one of my Oriental girls, and though she was a bit small for my personal tastes, I thought that her genuine charm and china-doll features would be most appropriate for such distinguished clients as Mr. and Mrs. Ambassador.

When we arrived, I was approached by a man who I thought to be the house guard. Suddenly I wanted to skip this assignment with the ambassador and start free-lancing. The guard was at least six feet four, a muscular man with gorgeous shoulders that formed a perfect V shape with his slender hips. Even though he was wearing a conservative gray suit, I could tell he was well hung. Concerning penis size, I usually like them so big that they're unsafe at any deed. You know, the kind of man you see on the street and wish he'd just take you right on the spot. When he opened his mouth, I practically died. Indeed, it was the male secretary—that same low and husky and sexy voice.

"Miss Hollander?" he asked. I nodded, weakly. "Oh yes," he said, bowing slightly. "She is waiting for you in the upstairs bedroom. The ambassador will be with you later. Will you follow me?" That isn't all I'd like to have done—but back to business.

Upstairs, Mrs. Ambassador was lying on an oval bed with a mirrored headboard. Somehow I always thought that a diplomat's bedroom would be different—conservative and respectable. Their sex lives may be as kinky as hell, but the bedroom should at least be old-guard reserved. I just wasn't ready for the oval bed, the mink bedspread, the mirrored headboard, and the red lights in the Tiffany lamps. And there she was wrapped in black satin sheets, the diplomat's wife, lying motionless on the oval bed. I wouldn't have been surprised if it had started revolving while strains of "Strangers in the Night" came from the background.

The secretary left the room, silently closing the door behind him. Usually the paying customer asks the prostitute's name and offers her a drink, making some chitchat before they get down to business. Not Mrs. Ambassador. I was pretty sure I'd been invited to this place for sex, but now I was beginning to wonder. I was used to strange setups, but this was getting stranger and stranger. Finally, I noticed she was beginning to move. Where her legs had been covered in black satin sheets, they were now bare and open so that her crotch was completely exposed to us. I noticed that her pubic hairs were shaved into a heart shape. Looking closer, I also noticed that her crotch was quivering ever so slightly. I then realized what a really trim, beautiful body she had; such flawless milk white skin I'd never seen.

Even though the diplomat himself was a bit old for me, I was hoping he'd make an appearance so that we could get the old ball rolling. So far, however, he was nowhere in sight.

I tried introducing myself to the quivering body on the oval bed, but there was still no response. Suzi walked over to the bed, kissed the woman softly on the lips. No answer. I tried the same, but nothing. By now I was getting a little pissed that I was being given no directives and really not shown much interest.

At that point the door to the bathroom opened, and in walked Mr. Ambassador, wearing a red kimono with fiery blue dragons embroidered on its sleeves. I nodded to him, almost in relief, when he made a rather vague twirling motion with his hand. "Would you please begin with my wife?" he asked, almost in a whisper, yet smiling. I expected him to join us, but instead, he took a seat in the far corner of the room, folded his hands, and gazed at us attentively. "Begin. Begin, please," he said breathlessly.

I looked at Suzi, took a deep breath, and directed my attention once again to the body on the bed. Indeed, she was beautiful. Her figure was so slender, with slim hips and practically no ass at all. And I'd never seen such milk-white breasts. Against the black satin sheets they looked even paler. They almost cried out for attention, some kind of loving caresses. I ran my hand around those fragile breasts, down her stomach and over her long legs just as Suzi's tongue dived right for her crotch. With my long red fingernails I began rubbing her feet, tickling her, trying to make the woman respond to my caresses. With Suzi's flicking hot tongue deep inside the woman's box and her hands caressing and pulling at the iceberg's thighs, I thought for sure Mrs. Ambassador would respond. Both of us wanted to arouse this woman in any way possible. If not sexually, then through some other sort of human reaction. I continued tickling her tootsies with my red nails. I had expected some outbursts of giggling, but instead, she broke out into the loudest, most uncontrolled orgasmic cry I've ever heard from any woman. Was it possible that within seconds she was already experiencing an orgasm? She'd seemed so cold and so unresponsive. How could this frigid woman suddenly be aroused to such tumultuous throes of sexual ecstasy?

With Suzi still performing cunnilingus on her, I directed my hands to the woman's breasts. Even though she was throwing her pelvis around in all directions—poor Suzi could barely keep her tongue inside the woman's vagina—Mrs. Ambassador's nipples were not erect. That was odd, I remember thinking. With my hands I twisted those brown candylike nipples between my experienced fingers. Still nothing. Kissing them with my lips, I spread some of my own saliva over her nipples and then tried working them again with my electric fingertips. I was so intent on making those nipples rise that I'd forgotten about there being anyone else in the room. It was then that I felt an erect penis glide against my legs.

I was on the bed, kneeling. I gasped immediately. Not only was I caught by surprise, but the man's organ felt particularly large and hard. My immediate fantasy was that the diplomat's male secretary had entered the room and taken me without a word. Closing my eyes, I reached out and felt the most incredibly large, balloon-like head I'd ever held in my hands. God, his balls were even large and firm. I slid him into me, twisting my crotch around, gripping this young stud's organ in my clutches. It felt so big in me that every thrust filled me completely, yet I wanted more. It was almost like an itch, an itch I wanted scratched and scratched again!

I felt his face against mine, but when I twisted my mouth to kiss his, I actually gasped out loud. I couldn't believe it! I was being made love to by a seventy-year-old man—Mr. Ambassador! He no longer seemed that twirpy little white-haired mouse I'd seen watching us a few minutes earlier. This old man couldn't have been more virile, and his body seemed young and strong and seething with sexual energy. One thing was for sure, too; he was screwing the living daylights out of me with a huge nonstop penis—and it was definitely attached to *his* body. No teenage boy I've made love to has ever had a harder or stronger organ.

When he let out a cry, I could feel his body twitch all over as the perspiration ran from him. I couldn't have held back even if I'd wanted to: I came with him—almost automatically. Exhausted, I pulled my hips from him so that his penis would dislodge. My God, his penis was still erect!

He immediately mounted Suzi and took her just as he'd taken me—doggy-style from the rear. And it wasn't a short session with her either. He grappled with her for at least a good twenty minutes. Meanwhile, Mrs. Ambassador continued in her orgasmic throes. Where Suzi had left off, I continued by massaging her clitoris with my tongue. It was then that I freaked! Her clitoris wasn't even hard. Screw her! I directed my attention at Suzi and the diplomat and the way his big erection slid in and out of her vagina. Her face was practically contorted in its ecstasy as she slammed her crotch against his organ, meeting every thrust of his head-on. But as I said, his wife was another story.

When Mr. Ambassador finished with Suzi, he politely thanked us for coming, put on his red Oriental robe, and left the room. His wife immediately stopped her orgasmic cries. Her body stopped writhing, and she pulled herself away from us, covering her body with the black satin sheets. "Please, please go," she whispered. And so we did—gladly.

I performed these little rituals with Suzi whenever Mr. Ambassador was in town. After about our sixth session Mrs. Ambassador finally leveled with us, asking us if we couldn't go a bit easier with our lovemaking. "I'm not a lesbian, you know," she said, turning slightly pink in embarrassment. "That's just my husband's fantasy."

So, this virile old codger not only fantasized that his wife was a lesbian, and forced her to fake it in order to support his fantasy, but he also believed in the old myth that all prostitutes were gay. He'd hire them to play around with his beautiful wife, and then he'd take them for his own. Somehow it soothed his ego to think that he could make a lesbian experience orgasm through heterosexual sex. His fantasy was for him to be the superman: the man who could make a lesbian come. While I'd never had better septuagenarian sex, the old man's idea of a ménage-à-twat was a bit much—even for me.

Caper No. 5: The Virgin Springs, or A Bedding in White

Very few wives of political bigwigs have to play the role of a "fantasy" lesbian, I'm sure, just to support their husband's illusions. One official in the Transportation Department turned out to be one of the most bizarre hard-core lesbians I'd ever encountered, in bed or out.

It was rare that as a prostitute I'd ever receive a phone call requesting exclusively lesbian sexplay. Gay women tend to be a very discreet lot and generally keep their lovemaking very private and payment-free. Only one call girl I know of—Laura, a beautiful black courtesan whom I wrote about in an earlier book—actually specialized in servicing lesbians. As I wrote in my first book, she used to lay Mrs. Showbusiness, as well as a number of other famous gay women, with a doubled-headed dildo. Laura actually became known within the business as the "gay courtesan," so popular was her technique with the lesbians.

I had once laid Mrs. Showbusiness myself, as favor to Laura. But it was a real freak scene, and I was hesitant when Laura called me just a few weeks later.

"Xaviera, please, you've got to do me another favor," she began. I took a deep breath. Laura was such a beautiful chick—and an even better lay. I wanted to help her out, but these freaky sex scenes were more than I could handle. Still, the voyeur in me finally won out. No doubt she'd want me to have bizarre sex with some celebrity.

"Okay, Laura, what's up this time?" And I was positive it wasn't some guy's penis.

"Xaviera, I've already promised this movie actress that I'd accompany her to Acapulco for the week. Wouldn't you know"—she laughed, obviously stalling for time—"Mrs. Trucker just flew into town from Washington and needs to be serviced."

"So take her to a garage," I suggested with a chuckle. But Laura finally convinced me that she really needed help. "Please, Xaviera," she pleaded, "just this once. It's a quick four hundred dollars."

Four hundred dollars! What did this woman want for service? A complete overhaul? As it turned out, I wasn't entirely wrong.

XAVIERA'S FANTASTIC SEX 207

The following evening—equipped with a man's tuxedo and a large strap-on plastic dildo in my oversized handbag—I proceeded to call on Mrs. Trucker. Hers was certainly one fantasy I thought impossible to materialize. As they say, you can't carry me back to old virginity. But they were wrong!

Her apartment was on Central Park in one of the city's most exclusive buildings. I'd heard so much about this building that I was expecting to be treated to a view of expensive antiques, Oriental carpets, and Art Deco delights. While I was the happy hooker, I always told my mother that I was an interior decorator, and it certainly was a pleasure to visit wealthy people's beautiful homes. Maybe I'd missed my true calling after all.

When Mrs. Trucker opened the door, I was greeted by a middle-aged, rather plump woman. Still, she was handsome in a maternal kind of way. She guided me to the bedroom, pointing out various artifacts and souvenirs of her world travels as we exchanged pleasantries. She seemed gracious, and her apartment was exactly what I'd expected. Yet something was wrong. It all seemed artificial somehow and very unlived in. I couldn't quite place my finger on what was wrong.

Then I noticed the squishing of plastic under my feet. *That* was it! Everything in the room was covered in clear plastic, the kind of plastic some housewives use to protect their furniture from dirt and little children. This woman, though, was covering her priceless antiques with it. There were plastic strips to walk on, plastic on the oak coffee tables, plastic on the gold brocade draperies—plastic *ad nauseam*. Either this woman was a cleanliness freak or she had a very serious plastic fetish. From the looks of things, it was probably a combination of the two.

When we got to the bedroom, Mrs. Trucker excused herself, saying that she had to make herself "comfortable." I took that as my cue to don the tuxedo. Laura had directed me to strap on the dildo so that it would stick out through the fly. Looking at myself in the mirror, I almost burst into laughter at the outlandish sight.

"I'm ready now, dear," I heard from over my shoulder.

I turned around, and there before me was Mrs. Trucker, dressed in a white floor-length wedding gown with a lace train—and a cutout crotch. Laura hadn't told me about this! Her instructions were for me to make love to a woman who fantasized herself as a virgin, but she hadn't said anything about her being a virgin *bride*! No wonder I was wearing a tux. What next? I thought. Would she play "Ave Maria" on the stereo and burn incense?

"I'm waiting, dear." Her voice was high and girlish now, and from the look of her naked crotch, she wasn't just waiting for breakfast in bed.

"I've kept myself pure just for you," she whispered, "just for this night, our first night together."

Laura should have been more honest with me. I tried playing along with this woman's fantasy, so I mumbled something about how I couldn't wait any longer to make love to her, how much I wanted her. "This must be obvious to you," I said, grabbing the head of my plastic dildo. She looked at my "erection"—my God, it was plastic, too!—and let out a soft sigh.

After a very long silence Mrs. Trucker asked me to carry her to the bed. I immediately began stripping the white satin gown from her body—Frederick's of Hollywood, no doubt—when her hand caught mine. "Please, let me keep it on," she said. "I want to remember this moment with my white dress on."

She could do what she liked with her dress. My tux was rented, and I thought it best to strip. Then I proceeded to mount my "bride" on the bed, but there was a strange crackling noise. Could it be she even had plastic under her white linen sheets? Ignoring the sound effects, I plunged my ten-inch plastic dildo into her waiting vagina. (Remember, the dress was crotchless.) It was obvious from the ease with which I was able to apply my dildo that this woman had either had many men or many dildos, no doubt mostly the latter.

I whispered sweet-nothings in her ear as I thrust my plastic penis into her repeatedly. "My God," I moaned, shoving the dildo even deeper into her, "I can't believe how tight you are."

"You are my first, my first," she cried as the dildo slid in even farther.

"Am I hurting you?" I asked.

"I'm O.K.," she reassured me. "Please don't worry."

"Are you all right?" I asked, noticing that all ten inches had disappeared into her.

"Yes. Oh, darling, make love to me."

"Oh, I love you so much."

"I'm so glad we waited," she moaned. I noticed that her fingers were on my clitoris, twisting it between her fingertips. "I'm so glad that I remained a virgin . . . for you."

"I love you," I said, sighing, and then I withdrew practically the entire dildo and sunk it back into her—all ten inches.

"For you," she screamed, "I remained a virgin!"

Even though I made love to this woman for nearly an hour, she never experienced an orgasm. Finally, she asked me to stop.

"We can't expect too much our first time," she said, smiling slightly. "Maybe some other night we'll experience complete ecstasy," she said. She then asked me to leave.

I somehow felt I'd been had as I left the apartment. She had paid me the four hundred dollars, yes, but my ego had been crushed. Strange as it sounds, I felt like some poor male lover who couldn't satisfy his woman.

When I talked to Laura a week later, she apologized for not telling me about the wedding dress. Still, she had to laugh at my story.

"Don't feel bad! It's merely part of her fantasy." Laura chuckled. As Laura told it, she had played out this woman's fantasy dozens of times. Each time was like the "first time" for Mrs. Trucker, and never did she experience an orgasm.

"She thinks she's a virgin bride," Laura explained. "Virgins just don't have orgasms their first time out."

"But how did she manage to hold back?"

"Don't ask me," Laura replied. "It's her fantasy—not mine."

Caper No. 6: The Washington Fairy-Go-Round

I met Gary when I first hit the singles' bar scene in New York City. He was handsome, built, black, and performing as a singer in one of my favorite pickup spots. Gary saw me there a lot, and I checked him out, but since he was gay, we just became good friends.

Before we met, Gary had put out a few singles, one of which even made the Top Ten for a month. Now, however, he was just a star fucker, someone who makes it with the real VIPs, or, as I call them, "the very impressive penises," and I'm not referring to genital size.

All his big affairs had been with famous men: a well-known radio and TV disc jockey, a Broadway choreographer, a wealthy interior decorator, and now a U.S. congressman. (Obviously, Gary's taste in lovers was on a downhill slide.) Not only was Gary a star fucker, but he specialized in white guys. In that sense, this U.S. congressman was perfect for Gary, since he loved making it with black guys. Perfect fantasy complements!

Gary's other fantasy, however, didn't quite mesh with Washington's closet mentality. You see, Gary also wanted a child, and the way in which he proposed to sire this child explains how I entered the caper.

One night I skipped out of my brothel to catch Gary's act down at Max's Kansas City, the "in" quasi-mixed singles' bar in Manhattan at the time. Gary had invited me there, saying it was important for us to talk after his gig. It was then that he told me about his sex fantasy, one that he now hoped to take beyond being a mere masturbatory dream for him.

"Xaviera, I've just got to be a father," he began. He was twiddling his cigarette nervously, and I could see how intense he really was about having a child. "I've thought this out carefully. I've even talked to you about it before."

"Yeah, yeah." I nodded. "But, Gary, you're gay."

"Okay, I'm gay," he said, taking another drag on his cigarette. "Okay, I've tried to screw chicks, and I've failed. I can get an erection, but just when I'm about to enter the girl's vagina, I always go soft. With guys I never have that problem."

"Yeah, and you can't have a kid from screwing some guy's ass," I commented.

"Please skip the biology class," he said. "Tell me, can you take two large penises at the same time? Both of them up your vagina?"

"I've done it before," I said, shrugging my shoulders. Modesty had always prevented me from boasting about this accomplishment.

"Fabulous!" he shouted. "Then you're it!"

"What 'it'?"

"I want this child, Xaviera," he said. His voice was lower now, more under control. He obviously meant business, and as he continued speaking, I could tell that this child fantasy of his was very real indeed. "You see," he continued, "I've planned it out this way. My lover, the one from D.C., and I will make love to you together. We'll put our erections in together and enter you at the same time. That way I'm sure I can keep myself hard long enough to enter you and impregnate your vagina with my seed."

Gary continued talking about how important this moment would be for him, how he wanted to share it with his lover. The child would be "their" child since they'd be screwing me at the same time. Unfortunately, Gary forgot to consider that *his* child would cost *me* a nine-month pregnancy. And as they say in the business, "A pregnant prostitute is a technological failure."

Of course, I rejected his proposal completely, but since Gary seemed so dead set on it, I promised him that I'd look around for some girl to have his/their child. And then I forgot about it. Quite by chance, however, a few months later I came across a girl in desperate need of money. Sherry was not exactly the brightest girl in the world—what smart girl would go in for a scene like this?—but she was attractive. Gary thought she was beautiful, but he wondered about her intelligence. So did I, but I assured him that intelligence was not inherited but was the result of environment. "Read B. F. Skinner," I told him.

The date was set, the money (four thousand dollars) exchanged, and a hotel room reserved. I promised to be there to supervise this great event. Congressman Straight, however, showed up drunk and high on about four Quaaludes. "It's the only way I could get him here," Gary confessed, trying to prop up his lover. Congressman Straight, however, was so stoned out of his mind that I doubted he'd ever be able to perform. Gary started sucking and tugging away at his cock; meanwhile, I went to work on the man's anus with my finger and tongue. The guy was gay, but he was so stoned I'm sure he'd didn't know me from a man or a kangaroo. Finally, he got something that resembled an erection, not exactly hard but reasonably firm.

When they were about to enter Sherry, I held back her lips to make for an easier entry. Unfortunately, these two men measured about eight inches around when their genitals were put together. I broke out some K-Y—by now I was feeling like a lewd Florence Nightingale—and greased them up good, telling Sherry to relax completely.

As I held her lips back again, Gary and the congressman entered her slowly but surely. Sherry didn't scream, but I could tell by the way she gripped my arm that it was a painfully snug fit. When the two men began thrusting their erections into her, she gripped me harder. After a few long, slow thrusts I could tell, though, that she was actually easing into the size of these two men. Having taken two men in my vagina at the same time, I knew what a peculiar feeling it was. Not only is it incredibly large, but you have this wild sensation of thrusts at different times and different rhythms.

By now Sherry was throwing her head around as though in convulsions, and I couldn't tell whether she was in pain or pleasure. Probably somewhere beyond. In about ten minutes it was all over. Gary shot his load first but remained in Sherry until Congressman Straight spent his. It always takes longer if you're stoned.

In two months Sherry reported that she was indeed pregnant. Gary then gave her another four thousand dollars. When the child was born, however, it was not a black baby. The child was white, Congressman Straight wanted nothing to do with it—actually, he never remembered the entire affair—and Sherry began proceedings on a paternity suit. The story was about to hit the press when blood tests showed that the child couldn't have been the Congressman's. You'd think that the rumors that circulated after this affair would have ruined his chances at the poll, but the results were altogether different.

For years rumors had circulated that Congressman Straight was a homosexual, and his rather conservative district was getting uppity until this rumored paternity suit hit. Even though it failed to make the papers and the courts, it gave the congressman an image of machismo, thereby restoring his masculine profile and renewing his voter support.

For Gary, however, his sex fantasy remained just that—a fantasy. And for me the affair was like a practical joke, a fairy-go-round ride I'd never take again.

VIII. Seven Fantastic Sex Scenes You Can Play

If you've read all my sex fantasies, yet still ask the question "But, Xaviera, how do you dream up all those wild sex scenes?" then I offer you one last resort: Games Fantasists Play. Included here are seven sex scenarios I've enacted myself, each of which will help get your fantasy life going.

Too many people simply can't get beyond the realm of ordinary sex. You know, making love with the same person (a spouse), in the same room (bedroom), with the same foreplay (kissing), in the same position (missionary), and with the same sex aids (none). If that's the syndrome your sex life has degenerated to, it's time you started looking into a few variations on the same old ritual. Good sex is merely a matter of experimenting with the right variables, such as different partners, places, foreplay, positions, and aids. And fantasizing is one good way to interchange and fill in those variables.

Take the sex games I've played with my friends and lovers. Naturally, the biggest thrill for me is the question whom will I be sleeping with tonight . . . or this afternoon . . . or this morning? (Who said you can only do it in the dark?) I once put love notes under a few doors in a Brazilian hotel, requesting the services of a specific gentleman. I didn't get my man; instead, I got twelve. Call it Xaviera Roulette. It works!

Voyeurism can also help your sex life, particularly if you're the object of some voyeur's attention. Part of the exhibitionistic fun is to write your friends, describing your escapades. I wonder how many postal workers have been turned on by my erotic postcards—orgasms and all.

Not that I think orgasms are everything. There's always foreplay, and although it rates second best, if your fantasy life is strong enough, foreplay can be enough. Like the time I came through my left big toe. (Don't forget, this is a book on fantasies.)

But nothing beats sexual intercourse. Of course, you can improve on it, as I did when I dressed in a mask and bird-woman costume and got laid in a standing position. The man didn't even know who I was, which certainly added to the excitement. I guess you could say my costume was a sex aid, but at the moment my favorite bedroom aid is a tape recorder. But that's another game altogether.

The key to any successful fantasy is the ability to mix your own sexual desires in the most bizarre combinations. The chemistry can be great if you just know how to play the game, and here are seven scenes to show you the way.

Fantasy Scene No. 1: The Masquerade Ball

When people think of fantasy games, they immedately imagine some wild orgy. True, group sex can work by allowing people to lose their inhibitions and enact those sex fantasies they'd only dreamed of. Yet some people, like my bashful rubber fetishist friend Peter, need something to help loosen those inhibitions—even at a sex party. Booze can help, but alcohol also tends to lower a man's staying power, and what good are uninhibited men if they can't get it up?

By accident I came across one of the best solutions toward lowering people's inhibitions. And it's fun, too. I was at the Carnaval '77 in Rio de Janeiro and living with a Brazilian architect named Luiz. We hadn't met before my arrival in Rio, but my Italian friend Pietro had written a letter to Luiz, a friend, that Xaviera Hollander was going to be visiting Brazil. Pietro had mentioned his name to me many times, and I considered looking him up when I got to Brazil. How surprised I was when Luiz called me all the way from Rio de Janeiro, inviting me to live with him during the carnival.

Flying down to Rio, I had all these marvelous fantasies about this tall, dark, handsome Brazilian meeting me at the airport. In fact, over the phone his voice sounded like that of a black, and I kept wondering if I'd be sleeping with a black man for the next few weeks. But Luiz was not black, and although I wasn't exactly disappointed, I had so visualized him as a black in my mind that when I saw the man, I just screamed out, "My God, you're not black!"

Luiz took a few steps back. "Well, I'm sorry to disappoint you. If I knew you wanted a black man, I'd have made the necessary arrangements."

I laughed and simply explained my impressions of his voice over the phone. Luckily enough, Luiz was no disappointment himself. He was a tall man with a muscular body, of Indian origin, rather macho-looking. Like so many Brazilian males, his masculinity gradually won me over. If I were to say what finally made me so attracted to Luiz, I'd have to say it was his eyes. Oh, those dark, penetrating Portuguese eyes of his! Often, I'd find myself hearing Luiz speak, yet not listening to him at all, but rather peering into his eyes. Sometimes Luiz would even catch me staring at him and say, "Are you so bored? Aren't you listening to me?" Of course, I wasn't bored at all, and I'd have to look away, blushing in embarrassment.

At first it didn't bother me that Luiz was married. Luiz and Vivienne, his wife, were great hosts, and it was quite common for a number of guests to stay all night in their large apartment in the elegant district of Leblon in Rio. While I was there, Vivienne spent a number of nights with her various male houseguests, but strangely enough, Luiz kept away from other women; he slept either with Vivienne or alone. Certainly his wife was uninhibited enough, and there were plenty of available beautiful women.

I had been staying with Luiz for only a few days when he invited me and his other houseguests to a masquerade party in a huge, privately owned mansion in the mountains. I really didn't take the costume part of the ball very seriously. I thought a tiny black mask covering my eyes would be sufficient, but when Luiz asked me what person, animal, or thing I was going to be for the ball and then showed me his elaborate nineteenth-century African safari-hunter costume, complete with rifle and pince-nez, I knew I'd have to come up with something very special and different.

But what? I was sure everyone would expect me to wear a very sexy outfit, but I wanted to surprise them. And the costume ball was only a day away! I rushed to a dressmaker and gave her my designs for an incredibly outrageous costume. Since this was a rush order, I had to pay the woman quadruple, but it would be worth the extra cost.

The night of the ball everyone wanted to know how I'd be dressed, but I told no one—least of all Luiz. Oh, especially not Luiz!

Of course, my entrance to the ball would be very important, so on the night of the party I showed up an hour late. The ball itself was a wild scene with a hundred people dancing their tits and asses off to the samba music of Brazil. Everywhere, costumed people were making out, kissing and grabbing at each other's bodies—bodies decked in costumes that seemed a cross between Las Vegas glitz and Amazon chic.

And then I walked in, gliding down the grand staircase, my seminude body covered in hundreds of blue feathers, most of which were on my face around my eyes. I looked like some tropical bird, and when a friend of Luiz's said, "Look over there, Luiz, your bird of paradise." Luiz looked at me with his safari rifle in hand, and I darted across the room. Oh, how I hoped he hadn't recognized me. What with all these feathers on my face—and a few thrown on my body for discretion's sake—I don't see how even my own mother would have known me. Not that I exactly wanted her to see me now.

Of course, the fact that my bird of paradise costume perfectly complemented Luiz's African hunter outfit was purely intentional on my part. He followed me across the crowded dance floor, but tonight I wanted to be the little tease, so I quickly asked a man in a Russian czar costume to dance with me. Luiz gazed enviously at my dance partner, just as I wanted him to.

I went from man to man that night, dancing with dozens of them, but never did I let Luiz get within arm's reach of me. He tried many times, and that's why I had to change men so often. I was sure Luiz didn't recognize me, though, because he kept asking other people at the ball who the bird of paradise was. But no one knew. He might have lost interest in me—I was such a tease—but I did my best to hold his attention.

As I've already stated, this costume ball was a very horny affair, and since I was wearing nothing more than a few plucked feathers, a number of men found it tempting to touch what lay under all my plumage. But I played it very aloof, and whenever someone went for my body, I dodged his hands just in time for him to feel but not grab. And it soon got around that the bird of paradise was one chick who could not be had.

Not that I didn't give every man in the place a chance to chase me. First of all, I was wearing just a few blue feathers over my crotch, one long one down the crack of my butt, and light-blue balls of puff around my nipples. My face, however, was covered in a mask of plumage, topped with a headdress of cascading ostrich feathers. I remember looking at myself in the mirror and thinking that I had worn all the feathers in all the wrong places, but that was the idea: to give all the people all the wrong ideas.

While I was dancing the samba, I'd keep myself at arm's length from the man I was dancing with. But as I danced I'd make sure to wiggle my ass and tail feather against the buttocks of the man or woman dancing behind me. Naturally, the person I was dancing with would be eyeing my nearly nude body, wondering what was beneath the feathers. Then he'd notice the action of my behind. Yet I'd keep him at a stiff arm's length. This went on for hours, but all the while I made sure Luiz was nearby, watching me.

A number of times he asked me to dance, but I always replied, *"Non, merci, plus tard, peut-être."* Of course, I knew Luiz spoke only very little French, but that was part of my disguise. How could he possibly recognize my voice if I were speaking a foreign language?

It was three o'clock in the morning. And there I was rubbing my ass up against the posterior of a man dressed as a bull-dyke policewoman while I danced with the tin man from Oz. Finally, I decided that I'd tortured and teased Luiz enough. I excused myself from the dance floor and walked over to the terrace door, as though I were trying to catch a breath of the cool evening air. I caught Luiz's eye, and as I turned to walk outside, I kept my eyes in his direction as if to say, "Follow me, please."

There was a slight breeze, and it blew the white draperies of the ballroom as the orchestra played on and on. I stood on the terrace for a moment. Of course, there was a full moon with tiny slivers of clouds passing over it. Too much moonlight, actually, for my disguise. So as Luiz followed me, I walked into the tropical garden below the terrace, where it was darker and more private. Oh, how Hollywood, I thought.

I kept looking at Luiz all the while, and naturally he pursued me. And then, underneath a eucalyptus tree, I turned and faced him at last. "I have been waiting for you." I spoke with a slight German accent à la Dietrich, to confuse him even further.

"I thought you were French!"

"Vy, no, vat ever gave you dat idea?"

He looked at me closely and laughed a breathless giggle. "Why don't you take off your feathers?"

"Vatever you like." And so I began to carefully pluck off the puffs of feathers around my nipples.

"No, I mean the mask of feathers on your face!"

"You mean, you don't vant to see me naked?" I asked as I dropped my tail feather. "Don't you?" I pressed my naked breasts up against his chest. "I vouldn't mind seeing you naked." His crotch was bulging now, so I dug into his white safari pants and brought his penis out into the open. "Vy don't you vant to see me?"

"Oh, but I do. I do! You have a very nice body." He trembled.

"Vould you also like to feel my body?" With my hands I slowly placed his erection between my legs. "Like thees?"

"I'm married, you know." Luiz was so nervous his cock shook.

"So?" We gazed at each other momentarily, and then I took his rifle from him and placed it on the grass. "I'd rather ve use your own gun."

"But who are you? Please let me see your face."

"No, I can't. You mustn't look at my face. It is better this vay." With his erection still between my legs, I gradually opened my thighs and let his penis flip up into my vagina. "Oh, take me. I'm yours."

"But who am I taking?" His eyes looked frightened.

"Does it really matter?" Oh, his penis felt so good inside me. Inside me at last! I'd finally seduced this married man, whom I'd wanted for days. I couldn't believe that I was now holding his warm male organ in my very own body, but there it was, nervous but throbbing.

"Please, tell me your name."

"Let it be a secret. Let our love be a mystery." My body and mind felt uncontrollable now. I was some other person. A bird of paradise perhaps. A sexy vamp from an old movie. I didn't know, but I liked this play-acting. I liked the mystery of it, and the control it gave me over Luiz. But also, I wanted to know if Luiz would have enjoyed sex with Xaviera Hollander. Or was he merely interested in this make-believe bird of paradise? I would have to test my own sexual prowess—without feathers.

I could feel that Luiz was beginning to approach orgasm. His moans of pleasure were becoming quicker and quicker, and I could feel his penis throbbing even more violently inside me.

"Luiz, it's me. Don't you know who I am?" I'd dropped my German accent by now. "Hold me even tighter, Luiz. Hold me even tighter so that I can come with you." I pressed my thighs together, harder and harder, and Luiz drew me closer to himself. And as he did, I slowly lifted off my feather headdress.

He gasped for breath when he saw me, and in the middle of what seemed like his orgasm, Luiz screamed out my name. "Xaviera ... Xaviera...."

He screamed it so loud that I came with him. I really wasn't ready to climax, but somehow his excitement and surprise were absolutely contagious. I don't think I've ever known a man's penis to change in midvagina, but Luiz's certainly did. When he first saw my face, he practically pulled out from shock, but as Luiz gradually realized who I was, he sank it back into my body and let his gorgeous orgasm complete itself.

Luiz told me afterward that he had never been unfaithful to his wife before. "Vivienne sleeps around, I know. I prefer she not do so, but it is her life, and I'm not like all these other possessive Brazilian men. But somehow my Catholic upbringing has prevented me from having extramarital sex."

"Then why me tonight? Or should I say, the bird of paradise?"

"I guess it was your costume, the mystery of not knowing who you were. Don't get me wrong. I find you very attractive. I wanted you even when I first met you at the airport. Still, I had no idea we'd ever ... ever actually—"

"Ball?"

"Ball? What do you mean—*ball*? Like *baile*, a party? A costume party?"

"Well . . . yes, I guess you could call it that. A masquerade ball."

Fantasy Scene No. 2: A Love Letter to Twenty Strangers

Do you remember passing notes in class to a young sweetheart? It may seem a little adolescent, but sending love notes is a favorite fantasist game for adults—if you play it right.

While in Rio for the Carnaval, I stayed with a girlfriend, Marcia, in the Copacabana Hotel. A sporty-looking, beautifully suntanned man stepped into the elevator with me, and during our brief ride from the ground floor to the tenth floor, we struck up a conversation. I asked him where he was from, since he spoke fluent English but with a slight accent.

"I'm from Israel," he said with a smile. "And you?"

"Well, I'm from Holland, but actually I just came from your country. I was traveling in Israel for about one month. I love the Israelis; they are very handsome, brave people."

The man laughed and asked if I was Jewish.

"Well, only half. My dad was a Jew."

Then the elevator doors opened to the tenth floor, and my Israeli walked out. I didn't even have a chance to get his name. I told Marcia about the nameless Israeli I'd just seen and talked to on the elevator. Suddenly I got an incredible idea for a superb fantasy game. Since I remembered the Israeli's floor, and since there were only twenty rooms on each floor, why not write twenty little notes, each of which would have the same message:

> Shalom! If you are the gorgeous man I met on the elevator this morning, please get in touch with the Dutch woman in Room 2407. Or meet me at the swimming pool downstairs. Or at least leave your name and room number at the desk.
> X. Hollander

Marcia and I repeated the notes and slipped them under every door on the tenth floor.

A couple of hours later, after Marcia and I had devoured a voluptuous buffet lunch, we went to the pool, stretched out on our mattresses, and waited for my Israeli idol. We weren't there for fifteen minutes when I spotted my mysterious elevator mate.

"Shalom! Shalom!" I shouted, waving my hands frantically at him. "How are you? Do you remember me?"

The Israeli took off his sunglasses and squinted in my direction. At first I was afraid he didn't remember me at all. How disheartening, but then he smiled a look of instant recognition and walked over.

"I couldn't quite see you with all this brilliant Brazilian sun in my eyes. How are you? I'm Noah."

Oh, a biblical name, I thought. How romantic. "Good morning, Noah. I'm Xaviera. And this is Marcia."

"So what are you doing here in Rio? Vacationing?"

"Well, not this instant, actually. I'm writing a book, among . . . other things." I paused significantly between the words "among" and "other things."

"So you're an author. What books have you written?"

"Seven books, exactly. This will be my eighth. My first was called *The Happy Hooker*."

"The Happy Hooker?" My Israeli paused for a second, turned his eyes away slightly, and said, "Well, I do know what *hooker* means, of course." And as if to protect himself, Noah pointed to a woman wearing white zinc oxide and a nose protector. "I'm just vacationing here in Rio with my wife. She's sitting over there by the pool."

"The one with the nose?"

"Yes, that's her." And my potential Israeli lover—whose potential had suddenly vanished like a puff of smoke—called his wife over. Another sex fantasy ruined! What was worse, I had to make up some pleasant chitchat for a few minutes to cover my embarrassment. But a swimming pool makes a good escape hatch. I soon excused myself to dive into the pool to "cool off."

You may think, after reading of my experience, that leaving notes is a no-win fantasy game. I was beginning to think so too until about an hour later when the bellboy circled the pool, paging Room 2407. I waved and the bellboy gave me a letter, a note from a tall, handsome Austrian man who occupied Room 1020 but who just happened to be sitting only two beach chairs away from me.

And then, not ten minutes later, I received a note from a wealthy Texan who was waiting for me upstairs in Room 1011 with an offer of five thousand cruzeiros—if I'd spend the night with him.

And a note from a lovely teenage girl in Room 1015 who said to meet her for a swim later that night.

As games go, this one went surprisingly well, with

more surprises than any one woman could possible handle.

Well—any woman except Xaviera.

Fantasy Scene No. 3: Sleepytime Sex

I had spent a few weeks in Amsterdam with a young Dutch ballet dancer named Richard. He was a good, strong lover but a bit naïve when it came to anything kinky or unexpected. So far he'd only had very jealous and possessive girlfriends, and certainly no one nearly so generous as myself.

Richard and I had known each other for a couple of months when I got a phone call from a homosexual girlfriend named Lisa inviting herself to visit me in Amsterdam. I couldn't have been more delighted. "You're in for a treat," I told Richard. "Lisa lives in Canada, and she's been going with the same woman for over a year. Unfortunately, Lisa is terribly faithful, and she prefers chicks, but every once in a while the girl needs a good cock inside her. Richard, it's time you started swinging a little."

Richard blushed. He was *so* inexperienced. What I didn't tell Richard was that Lisa's girlfriend, Marilyn, was so deathly jealous that no man would ever dare approach her.

Lisa and I had once been in love, and so when she arrived, we immediately ran into my bedroom to make love. She didn't know Richard was in my apartment at the time, and I didn't tell her. Of course, it was great sex because we hadn't seen each other for almost a year. Our lovemaking was the kind of sex where you tear and claw at each other's body, unable to get enough satisfaction, yet, you're just completely fulfilled after an hour of wild, horny wrestling in bed.

We talked for a while, but Lisa was very tired from her plane trip. Before she fell asleep, however, Lisa told me, "I still love you so much, Xaviera, but by God, I wish I could get screwed by a man. My girlfriend, Marilyn, is so damned possessive. I need a good cock again. Since I've been living with Marilyn, I've had absolutely no men."

"Look, dear, you just go to sleep," I said. "You're still recovering from jet lag, and you need to rest. Don't worry about your man. I'll come up with something."

She then put her head on the pillow and fell asleep instantly. I went into the next room and found Richard quietly reading a book.

"Richard, I want you to go into the bedroom where Lisa is sleeping and screw her. This is your chance to start swinging."

"You really mean it?" he said, and his book fell to the floor. "What am I supposed to do? What if she gets mad and throws me out?"

"Hell, boy, go into that bedroom and screw her!"

"But she is a lesbian, no?"

"Don't worry. She needs cock, too. Once in a while, at least. Just don't talk to her. Screw her while she's sleeping. Lisa hasn't had a good cock for over a year."

Well, I could tell that made Richard very hot. Like so many straight men, Richard wanted to give a lesbian some good dick and make her like it. "Just go into my bedroom and make love to her," I repeated. I guess he couldn't quite believe his ears, but gradually he came to his senses.

So Richard tiptoed in. I stood by the door and opened it just a crack, enough so I could hear them make love. Richard must have entered her immediately. I could hear Lisa's moans of ecstasy and the squeaking of the bed. Richard began gently enough, but soon he was screwing her full force. From the sound of it, Lisa was certainly enjoying Richard's lovely prick to the hilt. As he told me later, Richard grabbed Lisa from the back and penetrated her vagina from the rear position and screwed her that way because she was still soaking wet from my sucking on her pussy.

After Richard finished and left the room, Lisa slept for a few more hours. When she finally woke, there were a few visitors in my living room. From the looks of things, it was going to be a very interesting and horny evening—with or without Lisa's company. Finally, however, she did make an appearance, still slightly hung over from her long sleep. Lisa said her hellos, and then she sat down beside me and whispered, "Xaviera, I believe I got fucked so beautifully by some guy, but I'm not even sure whether it really happened or not. Maybe it was just a dream. I never even saw my lover. He took me by surprise."

Then Richard walked in with a trayful of coffee and cake, and recognizing him by sheer intuition, since she had never really seen him, Lisa shouted, "By God, it must have been you!"

Richard practically dropped the tray. My bedroom had been pretty dark when he took Lisa, and he was just now getting his first good look at the girl he'd made love to that afternoon.

Fantasy and reality—a little of each makes the sexual chemistry simmer. As Lisa put it, "Thanks for the wet dream!"

Fantasy Scene No. 4: Raped by a Tape

Surreptitiously taping conversations à la Watergate isn't exactly in vogue, but as long as you're the one with the recorder, it can be a fun fantasy game. Just destroy the tapes when you're finished.

Using a tape recorder in the bedroom takes a bit of preparation, and I don't mean just buying the right kind of batteries. If you want to tape your lover and you in intercourse, then I suggest you begin with some good marijuana. Generally, I don't care to use any kind of alcohol or marijuana to relieve one's inhibitions, but a little smoke can help loosen a person's tongue. This game takes expertise in a different kind of oral sex.

Once you're both in the right mood, you go to the bedroom and mix verbal intercourse with the sexual. Of course, you don't tell the person that there's a tape recorder hidden next to the bed.

The grass will help make your partner more talkative, but you still have to lead the way with a lot of verbal foreplay. You'd be surprised how silent many people can be during sex. Either they don't say anything or they speak in whispers.

I still have the tape from my first spanking session with my girlfriend Brigitte. We were both fairly well stoned when the two of us crawled into bed. I flicked on the tape recorder.

Immediately I felt as though I had to put on a performance. The recorder was going, and what fun would it be to play back a blank tape? Perhaps Brigitte had smoked a bit too much, though, because she seemed terribly passive and not at all verbal. I had to do something or my fantasy game would be ruined.

"Oh, Brigitte, I love that smooth, beautiful ass of yours." And I slapped her gently across the cheeks, but making sure it sounded good and loud.

"Xaviera, that hurts. Don't."

"But why not? You know you love it." I whacked her again—a little harder (and louder) this time. Brigitte always did have a few hang-ups about getting spanked. I think she's always seen it as a form of rape, that somehow I was taking her by force. But that didn't prevent her from responding sexually to the SM effects of a good spanking.

I began wiggling my left index finger in her vagina. I was right; she was already beginning to get wet just from my slapping her buttocks. Then I slapped her again across the ass. "Oh, your white ass is turning pink, rosy pink."

"You're not going to really hurt me, are you?" Brigitte looked a little concerned by now.

"No, it's just a way of expressing my love." By now my own ass was up in the air as I began licking Brigitte's vagina. I remember thinking how good oral sex sounds on the tape recorder. You never really know how noisy lovemaking is until you tape it: the low, deep moans, the hissing sounds released when you don't think you can take any more of it, the soft, high sighs as your lover nears her orgasm, the quick-paced, short gasps for air. And, finally, the piercing cry of the climax itself.

I'd just started circling my tongue around Brigitte's tiny clitoris, flicking it gently with the tip of my tongue. She already sounded close to her first orgasm—I could tell by her rapid, short gasps for air—when *she* whacked *me* a good one right across the ass.

Now it wasn't uncommon for Brigitte to play the aggressor in bed. After all, she'd been my French teacher in secondary school, and occasionally we did enjoy assuming old roles—in bed. But never had Brigitte tried spanking me. In fact, I couldn't remember any woman ever having laid her soft white hands on my bare bottom before this.

"Why did you do that?" I cried, trying to hold back my shock. I really wasn't hurt. Just stunned.

"It's only a way of expressing my love, dear. Remember?"

And at that she whacked me another good one. Oh, how my buttocks tingled . . . and kept tingling as Brigitte continued giving me tingly slaps on the hindside. I resisted, and that made it all the more exciting. My body braced and arched, and Brigitte slapped me again and again. Finally, I grabbed her hands, and we tumbled together, right off the bed. Her hands free again, she continued spanking me, even as she rimmed my anus with her long, wet tongue. Oh, the sensations of her wetness and my burning skin. I kept moaning and sighing until I climaxed repeatedly. At first I really forgot about giving Brigitte her orgasm. Then I made up for it. And of course, I forgot all about the tape recorder, which was the best part of all. Nothing beats spontaneity.

When I played the tape back a week later for Brigitte, she couldn't believe it. "You mean, I really do say those things in bed? My God, I've never heard our orgasm before—and so . . . so simultaneous! Is it really high-pitched like that, and so loud?"

"I didn't even know you had an orgasm. I was so far gone."

Brigitte laughed. "Are you kidding? Don't you remember how we brought each other off with our tongues?"

I'd forgotten completely, but there it all was on the tape recorder: the slapping of our buttocks, the squeaking bed, and our piercing high-pitched orgasms.

You might think people would get angry, knowing that you'd taped their sex. A few do, true, but usually they get so horny listening to their taped orgasms that they can't help getting it on with you again—right then and there while listening to the tapes over and over. The fantasy element of taping sexual intercourse, however, doesn't arise until you play the tape for someone else, someone who wasn't present at the original taping. Since this third person has only the sounds of your lovemaking to consider, the physical aspect becomes a complete visual fantasy. Which can quickly lead to a realistic acting-out scene—right there in bed with you.

Fantasy Scene No. 5: How to Blow a Toe

Gloria's lover Jack, the man with the minuscule penis, was a master of a very special game, that is, the ability to transfer erotic sensations to any part of his body. Just masturbate his elbow, his thumb, or his kneecap, and he'd come.

It's a game for experts only, and I must confess I've

succeeded only once. Yet coming through your toe can be a highly rewarding experience. If you love fantasies, you should at least give it a try. Practice may not make you perfect; it just may make you. Period.

Before Lisa and Marilyn met and I was still seeing Lisa, the two of us rented a chalet for several weeks in Collingwood, Canada. Collingwood is a beautiful resort area in the mountains, about a two-hour drive from Toronto, and during the summer it's the perfect place for swimming and other outdoor sports like tennis and horseback riding. During the winter, though, it's a fabulous ski resort.

Lisa and I had been lovers for several months, and we were looking forward to our stay in Collingwood as a vacation away from the city and her work as a schoolteacher. We'd been together in Collingwood for about a week, though, when I began getting horny for a man. As much as I love women, occasionally I do need some male sex, one way or the other. I loved Lisa very much, but after a week of only a woman's body, I began developing a tremendous desire for a penis. I kept thinking how much I'd have liked a cock to use on Lisa. Or vice versa. Unfortunately, Lisa just wasn't into dildos, so there was no solution.

One afternoon I was feeling hornier than usual. I'd played a hot set of tennis, and after a refreshing dip in the pool I returned to our chalet and pulled Lisa over next to me on the bed. I was so relaxed that my libido was almost uncontrollable. We began touching and caressing each other very gently as only two women can. She kissed my back and breasts, and then she aimed right for my pussy with her tongue. Lisa was a great cunnilinguist, I must say, and she was about to suck me right out when I pushed her away, saying, "No, not today. Don't eat me yet. I'm not in the mood for that. In fact, my vagina is the last part of my body

XAVIERA'S FANTASTIC SEX

you are allowed to touch. Okay? Today I feel like being the man. Don't suck me off as though I were a woman."

Even though I wanted to be the male, I also felt like lying there in a passive, pleasure-receiving way. Usually, I was the aggressor, but right then I wanted to be the macho man with a pleasure-serving woman. Lisa would be my geisha girl.

And she was *that!* Lisa began kissing and sucking me all over. I hadn't told her about my desire for a penis, but while she caressed me, I kept thinking how I had to find some part of my body and transform it by means of self-hypnosis into a hard, throbbing penis. Lisa sucked on my nipples, my fingers, and my earlobes, and as she sucked and kissed, I tried concentrating all my erotic feelings into that one part of my body she was kissing. But no luck. It felt good but no different from her usual gentle, sweet kissing. Then she went down on my right big toe.

Lisa was kneeling on the bed with her tongue on my toe and her little plump ass up in the air. Her tongue was soon flicking away between my toes. It was a very intense kind of sucking, so intense it felt as though she were drawing all my bodily energies into that one big toe.

And every time Lisa wanted to stop working over my toe, I'd beg her not to stop.

"No, don't stop, please. Keep kissing my toe. It's driving me crazy."

By now I'd actually transformed my toe into an imaginary penis, and while Lisa continued sucking on it, I had to tell her my fantasy.

"Lisa, suck my toe like you'd suck a man's cock. My toe *is* a cock, a ten-incher, and I'm about ready to shoot. Yes, I'm about ready to shoot my sperm into your tender and loving mouth. Can you feel my toe pulsate like a penis. It *is* a penis. Take my sperm; drink it. Oh, my God, I'm ... going to ... come!"

I guess my fantasy really turned on Lisa because she began masturbating herself. But I didn't have to masturbate. I'd truly concentrated all my sexual energy into that one big toe, and I was experiencing an honest-to-God orgasm.

I lay back, hands behind my head, and my entire body began to shake. My nipples popped up, and I even felt goose bumps. Yes, this was a real orgasm, a clitoral orgasm, but my clitty remained quite untouched.

This is probably the most advanced fantasy game a woman can play. As I've said, I've experienced this kind of orgasm only once. And damn it, once is *not* enough!

Fantasy Scene No. 6: Coming Attractions

Hollywood has been called the dream factory, but it might be more accurate to call it the wet dream factory. If it weren't for sex in the cinema, Hollywood would certainly be an empty town. One of my favorite fantasy games is recall to mind some of the great erotic scenes from the films. Naturally, I'm always the heroine. Those are not necessarily the most explicit scenes—primarily the ones that suggest sexuality in the most ordinary of settings or through the most mundane activities. I love the eating scene from *Tom Jones*,

XAVIERA'S FANTASTIC SEX

wherein a horny Moll seduces Tom with an oyster in her mouth. Or what about Faye Dunaway playing an erotic game of chess in *The Thomas Crown Affair*? Perhaps my favorite is the wrestling scene in *Women in Love*.

Now I don't suggest you gather a group of friends together and say, "Hey, let's enact the lesbian tango scene from *The Conformist*." Rather, memorize your list of favorite erotic movie scenes, and when the occasion arises, you can slyly suggest to your friends that they enact the scene. They need not even know that you're the director and they're your actors. Let me give you an example.

It was one of those extremely hot August nights when my Dutch photographer friend Peter was visiting Richard and me in Amsterdam. Richard, who is very strong and always into physical games, suggested they do some Indian wrestling. The two men were wearing short-sleeved shirts, but after a few contests of locking forearms, they were already too hot to wear even their flimsy shirts. I can't tell you how excited I got watching the two of them, stripped to the waist, in face-to-face combat, their hands and forearms entangled in a struggle of brute strength, faces wet with perspiration, muscles tense and bulging. I was so aroused that I actually crossed my legs and started rubbing them together. It wasn't enough friction to make me come, but it sure got me good and horny.

I couldn't go on like this forever, though. I had to do something. Then it flashed on me. Why not have these two men enact the male wrestling scene from *Women in Love*? Naturally I didn't tell them anything about the movie or my idea. That would be my own private sex fantasy.

"Wouldn't you men be more comfortable," I offered, "if you took off *all* your clothes? We're all friends here, and it's so hot." They looked at me rather stunned. Either one would have stripped for me in a flash, but undressing in front of me and another man was different. So I decided to lead the way. First my top, then my jeans, and at last my panties. Me in the nude.

"Well, aren't you going to join me? It's really so much more comfortable." They looked at each other. Richard shrugged and started undressing. "Come on, Peter. It won't hurt you." Peter was always such a shy one.

I dimmed the lights a little, enough to make Peter a bit more at ease. Finally, he succumbed. What else could he do with my hands tugging at his belt and unzipping his fly?

The men started Indian wrestling again, but I wanted to get them into more physical games. "Aren't you a little tired of Indian wrestling? Hey, what about the match we had a few weeks ago, Richard, when I pushed you down and we rolled around on the carpet for what seemed like hours?"

At that I pushed Peter down to the floor and fell on top of him. I slapped my hands against his chest playfully, knowing that Richard might be ever so slightly jealous at my wrestling with Peter. And in no time Richard was on the floor with us. I let Peter play with my tits a little because I knew that would get Richard even madder. Not that he would actually try to hurt Peter. I wrestled to stay on top, and just as Richard was beginning to join our little fight, I untangled myself from both of them. And there they were, the two of them, wrestling on the floor like two naked animals.

Had there ever been anything more erotic than seeing their brawny legs wrapped around each other as though they were actually making love? And yet they were fighting, each trying to overcome the other's brute strength. The perspiration on their taut muscles was soon glistening in the soft light, and I looked to see if their penises had even the slightest angle of inclination. No . . . nothing yet, just two lovely bouncing cocks that needed a feminine body between them. But I wouldn't surrender myself, not yet. First I wanted to savor the excitement of their combat, to watch Richard as he sat on Peter's back like some wild, crazy cowboy. His hands were holding onto Peter's buttocks, and Peter's cock hung down long and soft beneath him. It was difficult to see who was winning, but one thing was for sure: The two of them had definitely conquered my body without even touching me. Oh, the sight of their twin asses, one on top of the other. Bulging asses attached to firm thighs. My own body had been between each of their thighs so many times. The two men who had made me feel so good so often, and now they were locked together without me.

Quickly I slid under their bodies and sucked Peter's cock until he was rock hard. Richard, watching me suck off his opponent, soon got hard, too. And there they were, my two fighting men with weapons of hard, firm flesh. Just as I'd always wanted them.

They say that lesbian lovemaking is a favorite turn-on for heterosexual men. Well, I think women should start insisting that their men fight for them more often. For me there is no more erotic sight than two brawny men in combat. And when you snuggle in between their hot and tired bodies after the fight, and you are being made love to by both men simultaneously, then you can re-create the fight all over again—but this time in the sweet heat of sexual combat.

Fantasy Scene No. 7: Xaviera's Mail-a-Tail Service

Hundreds of people send me letters every month, detailing their most personal problems, and I quoted a few in a previous chapter. I answer these letters because many people really are quite unknowledgeable regarding the mysteries and wonders of sex. The letters I enjoy most, however, are the ones detailing sex fantasies. Usually these people have absolutely no reason for writing me, other than to turn themselves on by turning me on. And that's what makes them so great.

Generally I don't write erotic letters. I may detail a great lay here or there in one of my letters, but usually I save my blue prose for publication. Why arouse just one person when you can get an entire country hot? Still, there was one time when I played the fantasy game of writing hot letters to a fare-thee-well.

I had been in Brazil last winter for only a few days when I decided to see some of the country outside Rio de Janeiro, and so I took a trip to Salvador, Bahia, which is to the Cariocas (inhabitants of Rio) what Puerto Rico is to the New Yorkers. It's the perfect beach resort: picturesque surroundings, green woods, and colorful flowers. And the people are among the most beautiful I've ever seen. One reason they're so attractive, I think, is that their blood is a mixture of Portuguese, black, and Indian. These mulattos are a very sexy people, and their sex drive is the strongest I've known—most probably because of the hot weather and their own hot blood.

I couldn't believe how beautiful Bahia was. I just had to write my girlfriend Brigitte a letter, telling her how fabulous this country was. I told her about the lovely market places and how I listened to folklorico music played on the barimbaus and the atabaque. Best of all, however, was watching two well-built blacks dance the Capoeira, a dance which depicts the slaves' defense against their white owners.

I was at a beach café writing my letter when I noticed a group of loudmouthed Brazilian playboys eating up practically every girl in sight—with their eyes, of course. They checked me out, but since I prefer being the chaser rather than the chasee, my glance strayed, instead, to a rather shy, intelligent-looking boy who was sitting alone on a blanket. He was not staring at the girls but reading a thick novel by one of Brazil's most famous authors, Jorge Amado. I really couldn't tell what he looked like since he was hunched over his book. Also he was somewhat disguised, wearing a large visor cap and dark reading glasses, and instead of the sexy tight briefs his fellow Bahians were wearing, the boy was clad in a colorful but loose-fitting pair of shorts.

I stopped writing my letter to Brigitte, and within the next few hours I met this boy and *really* had something to write about! Since Brigitte loves hearing my wild escapades, I resumed my letter to her that evening. And I didn't spare a detail!

"He was a beautiful boy," I wrote. "I couldn't see how he was actually built, yet I found his aloofness quite attractive. After about half an hour I went over to him and in my best Portuguese-*cum*-Spanish, I asked him to rub some suntan oil over my body. 'It's so difficult to put it on my own back,' I said. 'And I have such delicate skin.'

"The boy spoke quite good English, as it turned out, and he introduced himself as Carlos. When I told him my name, Carlos pulled a local newspaper out of his beachbag and showed me an article on my arrest of a few days earlier. You see, Brigitte, I'd not worn any underwear underneath my white see-through lace dress, and I was arrested in a shopping mall.

"Carlos pointed at the picture and laughed. 'You are quite a girl. Unfortunately, the authorities here are terribly conservative. I don't know if you've noticed, but there are hundreds of cars parked every night along the beach promenade with couples screwing in them. And the police protect them. But by God, don't talk or write about sex in this country. It's a taboo!'

"As Carlos told me about his country, the beach became more and more crowded, so I asked the boy if he had a car. 'This beach is simply too crowded,' I said. 'Isn't there a place with some more privacy?' "

Then I noticed I was running out of paper. In fact, I had room for only about a sentence more. Damn it, and just when the story was getting hot. Funny, I thought, my having to stop just when I was reaching a climax—I mean, when the story was reaching a climax. It was like one of those American soap operas, when they say, at the moment of greatest suspense, "Tune in next week for the next episode."

I hunted around in my hotel room for some more paper but couldn't find any. I was about ready to ring for room service, when I stopped. No, why not? I'll put a P.S. on the letter, saying, "More tomorrow," mail it off, and write Brigitte one horny episode every day. After all, I had about ten orgasms with Carlos that afternoon. Certainly it should be good enough for at least ten letters. It would be my concept of "Serial Sex"—erotica on the installment plan.

Letter No. 2: February 2

Dear Brigitte:

Remember, Brigitte, I'd just asked Carlos if there wasn't a beach with more privacy? Well, luckily, he had an old VW. The boy picked up my bag and towel, and we drove off to one of the most deserted beaches in Bahia. I forgot to tell you that when Carlos took off his "disguise," he turned out to be a very handsome young man in an intellectual sort of way. On the way we passed a lovely village called Itapoa where hundreds of people were dancing on the street in a festival called Festa de Largo.

"For us Bahians, every day is a holiday," Carlos told me, "and we are all in a real carnival mood. You know that the original Carnaval originates in Bahia. Rio is for the tourists."

We walked for a few minutes through the hot white sands of the beach until we found a secret spot between two big rocks. Yet, we were not totally alone. In the distance I could see people sporting around in the water.

I asked Carlos to rub some more suntan lotion on my hot body. By now I'd taken off my string bikini top and was about to discard my bottoms when Carlos begged me to stay at least partially dressed.

"One cannot do such things in Brazil. If the police find you, you'll get arrested."

"So what? One more time in the clinker won't hurt

me. There is nothing that gets me more excited than making love under the blue sky with white sands beneath me and a hot sun burning away on my titties and ass. Speaking of the sun, could you please rub some more oil on my back?" Wouldn't you think Carlos would throw away the bottle of suntan oil and just ravish me then and there? Little did I know what it takes to seduce a Brazilian boy!

Love,
Xaviera

Letter No. 3: February 3

Dear Brigitte:

Well, Brigitte, Carlos began massaging my back and shoulders, very gently and very soothingly. You can always recognize whether someone is a sensual person by the way he applies the suntan oil. If he does it softly and smoothly, you can rest assured that he will be a sensitive lover. But if the man just slaps it on your back and rubs the hell out of you, forget him!

Meanwhile, Carlos again took off his cap and sunglasses. This time I had a chance to notice that his chestnut hair was cut very short and showed some streaks of premature graying. Still, he couldn't have been over twenty. No, make that eighteen. He took off his shirt, and only then did I notice what a man he was. Carlos was exceptionally well built. But did he know how to use what he had? I could only wonder. And hope.

Love,
Xaviera

Letter No. 4 (postcard): February 4

Dear Brigitte:
While Carlos was rubbing in the lotion on my bottom, I turned onto my right side so that my buttocks were actually touching his still-covered crotch. By now I was so horny that I literally ripped open his pants and aimed for his beautiful cock. What? Not hard yet? Another homosexual? Or so shy that rape would be my only alternative?

Love,
Xaviera

Letter No. 5: February 5

Dear Brigitte:
Brigitte, Carlos was just shy. Only when he'd made perfectly sure we were alone did he consent to remove his shorts. I caressed his penis gently, rubbing my ass against his lap.

"I admire your ass," he said. "You have the perfect ass for our taste in Brazil. We love women with good, firm asses and cannot understand why American women always are on diets. The ass is our ultimate fantasy. Breasts are less important to us."

Well, I was ready and eager, but since I'm Dutch, I decided to tease him a bit more. I rubbed more lotion over his already-stiff member. It was as if I were molding his erect and throbbing cock into some kind of sculpture. The lotion, combined with a few grains of sand, made his stiff penis look like a great phallic masterpiece.

Then I noticed that there were some people in the distance, and they were approaching us. Would Carlos have the courage to take me, then and there before God and the whole wide world? The boy began to panic! And so I panicked—but for another reason. Was he going to leave me stranded without my first orgasm for the day?

Love,
Xaviera

Letter No. 6 (postcard): February 6

Dear Brigitte:

Naturally, Brigitte, Carlos was quite nervous as his eyes kept flashing between the people and my body. Fortunately, my body won out, and within seconds he was trying to enter me. I took him up front and started sliding his cock back and forth, rubbing it against my thighs.

I knew that the exhibitionism of our situation would make him even hotter, and so as soon as I knew the people on the beach were noticing us, I screamed, "Carlos, hurry up. They're coming. They're coming!" I couldn't have cared less, but in all the excitement, might Carlos lose his erection?

Love,
Xaviera

Letter No. 7: February 7

Dear Brigitte:

As you may or may not know, Brigitte, there is no nicer feeling than having a sexy man's cum running down your legs, mixing with the sweat and the suntan oil. After spilling his seed, Carlos quickly put his swimming trunks back on, and the two of us ran into the water. Since Carlos was only a teenager, he got another hard-on quite fast.

The water is always such a sensual medium, and as I rubbed my tits against his big chest and the waves flowed over our bodies, I could see that Carlos was soon hard again. I decided to blow him right there in the Atlantic Ocean. I didn't tell him my plans, but simply pulled down his shorts and took all his hard meat into my mouth. Just as he was about to climax, a huge wave tumbled over our entwined bodies. Would the force of nature ruin my act of fellatio? Would I drown with a teenage boy's hard-on in my mouth? Women have come to worse ends.

Love,
Xaviera

Letter No. 8 (postcard): February 8

Dear Brigitte:

I had trouble hanging onto his body, but I wanted him to come again. Even though the huge wave pushed us over, I hung onto his cock with my mouth and his sperm shot out over my face and into the Atlantic Ocean. But I was still horny, and what's to be done with a boy who's already come twice in one hour?

Love,
Xaviera

Letter No. 9: February 9

Dearest Brigitte:

We dragged ourselves onto the beach and rested for a few minutes. Later that afternoon we walked up the beach toward a grouping of high rocks. I noticed an adolescent black boy up on the highest rock. He was sitting there drinking from a coconut, and to give him a little show, I threw off my towel and stood there naked. I could tell that the kid was interested because he hid behind a rock, thinking that I wouldn't see him. But I knew he was there watching us.

Then I noticed that there were about ten black guys, talking and joking among themselves, on the other side of the rocks; unfortunately, they couldn't see us. Oh, just knowing that all those men were so close, and that this kid was watching me, I got incredibly horny. I began fantasizing that the black kid was masturbating, sticking his young little cock into the coconut he'd been drinking from and using it as an artificial vagina.

I guess the kid called to his friends because soon a number of the black men from the other side of the rocks came to watch Carlos and me.

Now I had to have Carlos again. Of course, since he'd already had two orgasms, it took him a bit longer to get hard this time, but with the help of some suntan oil and a few grains of sand between my fingers, I was able to bring Carlos to his third erection of the afternoon. By that time, as you can imagine, I'd had half a dozen orgasms myself. Carlos wanted it again, too, but why was he resisting me? Did his apprehension have anything to do with those ten big black men watching us? They looked friendly enough.

Love,
Xaviera

Letter No. 10 (postcard): February 10

Brigitte, you won't believe what Carlos said.

"No, no. If we start making love again, they'll come over here and rape you and I can't fight off ten black men."

I laughed. "But I'd love it. I'd love it."

So we had wild sex as the black men looked on. Oh, would they take the hint and take me, too?

Love,
Xaviera

Letter No. 11 (postcard): February 11

Dear Brigitte:
Unfortunately the group of black men never de-

livered the goods. They chickened out. But Carlos and I gave them the show of their lives.

Love,
Xaviera

The fantasy element in a game like this is achieved when the person receiving the letter tries to figure out what happens next. As Brigitte told me later, "You left me hanging there with every letter. I'd have to go into the bathroom and masturbate. Of course, I had you doing all sorts of wild and perverse things in *my* fantasies. I must confess, sometimes my sex fantasies were better than the next installment of your letters. Still, I loved them. And those postcards! By the time those got to me they were all stained and tattered. You must have turned on the entire postal system from here to Brazil!"

Well, I'm happy to have given all those postal people a treat. But why limit it to them when I can reach millions in a book? So now that's what I've done in this volume of sex fantasies. Only words, you say? Ah, but words inspire thoughts, and thoughts inspire deeds. It all begins in the mind, and now I've gone and filled that libidinous mind of your chock-full of Xaviera's best notions, fantasies, dreams, ideas, and feats of sexual derring-do.